D0536585

# AMERICAN LABOR

## FROM CONSPIRACY
## TO
## COLLECTIVE BARGAINING

# WORKING PEOPLE
# AND THEIR EMPLOYERS

Washington Gladden

*With an introduction by Leon Stein & Philip Taft*

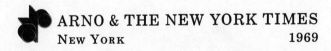 ARNO & THE NEW YORK TIMES
New York                                    1969

# INTRODUCTION

Washington Gladden was a Congregational clergyman who in a time of strikes and industrial strife in the United States sought a common ground for worker and employer. *Working People And Their Employers* was the first major book to expound the social gospel movement, a movement which sought to apply the fundamental principles of Christianity to the social problems of the day.

Gladden held a number of pastorates in New York, Massachusetts, and Ohio. Both as a speaker and as a writer he revealed his concern with the ethics of industry. He read widely and was familiar with socialist literature as well as with the basic tenets of classical laissez-faire political economy. The middle ground he sought adopted some, and rejected much, of each philosophy.

Unrestrained capitalism demonstrated its shortcomings in strikes, depressions, unemployment, hunger and shameful accumulations of wealth. On the other hand, socialism centralized power in the state to an oppressive degree. In *Working People And Their Employers* Gladden rejected unrestrained individualism, trade union interference and centralized state power. Instead, he offered a simple solution—appplication of the Golden Rule.

The solution of the labor problem required neither manipulation of the environment nor overthrow of the American system. Rather than plead for such materialistic or revolutionary approaches, Gladden urged the Christianizing of society.

The appeal, according to Gladden, must be made to the hearts of men and to whatever is in them that responds to something higher than the frantic urge to accumulate wealth. No external force, not even the state, can accomplish that change, Gladden believed, though in later books he recognized the creative social role of the state in initiating remedial legislation.

In the ten chapters of *Working People And Their Employers,* Gladden sought "to make it plain to working men that the religion of Christ is not hostile to their interests." He favored cooperative effort among workers and criticized practices aimed at restricting those efforts: While workers strive to achieve the benefits of cooperation, employers must curb their heartless, unethical individualism. Gladden emphasized the forecasts of political economists that the growth of capitalism will lead to "a harsh separation of classes, combined with those glaring inequalities in the distributions of wealth which most people will agree are among the chief elements of our social instability."

In 1905 Gladden castigated his church for accepting a $100,000 gift from John D. Rockefeller, a gift which he branded as "tainted" money. In an age of industrial strife and robber barons Gladden undertook a quixotic crusade for love and brotherhood, cooperation and temperance, mediation and Christian ethics.

*Leon Stein and Philip Taft*

# WORKING PEOPLE
# AND THEIR EMPLOYERS

# WORKING PEOPLE

## *AND THEIR EMPLOYERS.*

BY

WASHINGTON GLADDEN.

BOSTON:

LOCKWOOD, BROOKS, AND COMPANY.

1876.

*Stereotyped and printed by*
*Rand, Avery, and Company,*
*117 Franklin Street,*
*Boston.*

# PREFACE.

THE reader of these chapters will soon discover that they were written with an audience in view, and will infer that they were spoken from the pulpit.

It is not unlikely that some readers may pronounce discussions such as these quite too secular for Sunday and the Church; but the lawfulness of doing good on the Lord's day is not an open question; and the Christian who does not feel the need of trying to do good in this way, who does not see the importance of bringing the truth of the New Testament to bear directly upon the matters now in dispute between labor and capital, is one with whom I do not care to argue. Now that slavery is out of the way, the questions that concern the welfare of our free laborers are coming forward; and no intelligent man needs to be admonished of their urgency. They are not only questions of economy, they are in a large sense moral questions; nay, they touch the very marrow of that religion of good-will of which Christ was the founder. It is plain that the pulpit must have something to say about them.

If these lectures had been intended for students of political economy, some of the things here said might have been taken for granted ; but many of those to whom they were spoken were mechanics and operatives, who could not be familiar with all the current treatises on social science, and who therefore were not offended by instruction of a somewhat elementary character. I think I know my audience pretty well. The greater part of my life has been spent among working people, in working with them, or in working for them. I count among them some of my most valued friends ; I know their ways of living and of thinking ; and I have tried to make these discussions intelligible and helpful to them.

That any of the questions raised get their final answer in this book, I am not vain enough to imagine ; but I hope that it may help a little towards the understanding of some of them.

North Church Study,
Springfield, Mass.

# CONTENTS.

———◆———

# WORKING PEOPLE

*AND THEIR EMPLOYERS.*

# DUTY AND DISCIPLINE OF WORK.

To WORKING people and their employers these lectures are addressed; not to slaves and their masters; not to toilers and pleasure-seekers; not to workers and shirkers. It is not assumed that employers, or capitalists, or any other class of able-bodied adult persons in the community, are absolved from the duty of labor. The law which Paul laid down to the Corinthians, "If any man will not work, neither shall he eat," is morally binding upon Americans as well as Greeks. The fourth commandment is generally quoted as if it had exclusive reference to the observance of one day in seven as a day of rest; but it must not be forgotten that work is commanded by it just as explicitly. "Remember the sabbath day to keep it holy. *Six days shalt thou labor and do all thy work;* but the seventh is the sabbath of the Lord thy God; in it thou shalt not do any work." Resting on the seventh day is no more distinctly required than working on the other six days. It is not "Six days thou *mayest* labor," but "Six days thou *shalt* labor."

Thus in this compendious statement of moral principles given to the Hebrews at the beginning of their national existence, and intended to serve not only for the Hebrews, but for all races as a practical and sufficient rule of life, we find work enjoined as a duty; and no hint is given of any classes who are exempted from the command. The Ten Commandments are sometimes said to be the summary statement of the moral law: that which is required by them is moral; that which is forbidden by them is, in the most exact sense of the word, immoral. Idleness is therefore immoral; and whoever, man or woman, is living without occupation, is leading a life of immorality. A lazy man is not a moral man.

Not enough has been made of this clause in the commandment. We have often proved that idleness is inexpedient, that it is wasteful, that it relaxes the vigor of the body and the mind, that it is a deviation from the path in which He walked who said, "My Father worketh hitherto, and I work;" but we have not sufficiently emphasized the fact that it is an express transgression of the moral law, — in other words a sin, put by the divine Lawgiver into the same category with image-worship and blasphemy, and theft and murder and impurity, and sharing with these sins in the displeasure of God.

It hardly needs to be said that this rule of life, like every other, has its exceptions. Some persons are lawfully exempted from labor. The sick, the aged and infirm, infants, and the imbecile are not required to work. Ability always limits obligation. Whatever theories the theologians may have about it, God never expects of any one impossibilities. Young persons pursuing courses of education are also partial exceptions to this rule. They are preparing for work. It is not, however, well for them to be entirely relieved of labor. It is vastly better for their minds and for their bodies, that they should have some regular duties to perform outside the routine of school life.

I can think of no other limitations to the positive command, "Six days shalt thou labor." And it is high time that not only the dignity but the duty of work were enforced upon the men and women of our day. We had a battle to fight with the false philosophy of a former generation, in order to maintain the dignity of work. There were those who insisted that labor was dishonorable and degrading;

that the laboring classes ought to be servile classes.
That fallacy we have pretty effectually exploded,
though it took not a little gunpowder to do it. It
is now generally admitted in all parts of the land
that labor is honorable; that men, at any rate, are
not disgraced by it, however it may be with women;
that if any one chooses to work, rather than live on
the earnings of others, rather than beg or swindle
or steal, it is nothing against him. So far, so good.
But there is another step to take. Now we must
make it equally clear that labor is not optional but
imperative; that it is imperative, too, upon all men
and all women alike that have sound minds and
sound bodies; that it is not only respectable to
work, but that it is not respectable to be idle.

From the sentence pronounced upon Adam after
his transgression in Eden, " In the sweat of thy face
thou shalt eat thy bread," it has sometimes been
inferred that labor was the penalty of sin; that if it
had not been for the fall we should have subsisted
somehow without work. A most mischievous and
unwarrantable inference! Doubtless the tendency
of moral evil is to make work more difficult, hazard-
ous, and painful; doubtless the " whole creation
groaneth and travaileth " under its burdens of toil
as it would not have done if man had never sinned:
but if there were not, and never had been, moral

evil in the world, there would still be need of labor. For sinless as well as for sinful beings, work is the indispensable condition of development. Why, if you go back to the story of Genesis for your theories on this subject, please to remember that, before the fall, " The Lord God took the man, and put him into the Garden of Eden *to dress it and to keep it.*" No, work is no part of the curse. It is part of the original divine constitution. Laziness, — that is the curse. The terrible inertia of body and soul, the unwillingness to labor, which makes some men paupers, and some panders, and some swindlers, and some thieves, — that is the result of the fall, one of its worst and bitterest results.

By work, of course, I do not mean manual work exclusively. Hand work is just as honorable as brain work, and no more honorable. There is an infinite variety of work to be done, some of which requires almost no muscular exertion, some of which requires almost no thought, some of which calls for a combination of the powers of the mind with the powers of the body. And it cannot be denied that the tendency is to substitute mind for muscle in the various industrial operations of the period. In nearly every trade and calling, many things are now done by machinery that were once done by hand; and machinery is mind power substituted for muscle power. A machine is a contrivance of the human intellect by which some natural force or other — steam, or falling water, or wind, or compressed air, or electricity, or chemical re-action — is so directed that it does the work once done by muscular strength and skill. Vast numbers of our laboring people of both sexes now find their occupation in watching and tending these machines. Some manual labor is required, but the task is lighter. Doubtless these labor-saving machines will be constantly increasing in number and improving in efficiency, and much of the work that is now done by hand will be done twenty years hence by machinery.

In this tendency we see the working out of a principle which is fundamental in the plan of the Creator, — namely, that the natural comes first, and afterward the spiritual. There is a constant movement toward the substitution of intelligence for brute force. The cruder and coarser methods and processes are gradually supplanted by those more intellectual. Mind steadily gains on muscle, and will continue to gain until the spiritual or immaterial part of man shall obtain a complete ascendency over the natural forces of the world in which he lives.

This is certainly part of the divine plan; and working-men should understand it, and cease to quarrel with it. The steam-engine, the spinning-jenny, the power-loom, the power-press, the sewing-machine, all these mechanical devices by which labor is saved and production increased, are provided for in God's design. They are part of his great work of development by which he is carrying the race forward to its perfect destiny. They are not, as some working-men seem inclined to think, inventions of the Devil : they are the handiwork of God, just as really as the flowers and the grains that grow on the face of the earth, or the coal measures that are hidden beneath its surface.

I have sometimes seen the Scripture text, "These are parts of His ways," inscribed upon the walls of a cabinet of minerals or a museum of natural history; but it might just as reverently be written over the entrance to the machine-room of the American Institute, where the thoughts of God unfold themselves in the contrivances of men.

The men of the Bible were not all specially inspired men. There is no reason to suppose that Abraham or Jacob was inspired in any other sense than you or I may be. But there were a few men to whom (the record tells us) God did give a special inspiration. Among them was Bezaleel, the son of Uri, the son of Hur, of the tribe of Judah. "See, I have called him by name," says Jehovah; "and I have filled him with the spirit of God in wisdom and in understanding and in knowledge." And what was Bezaleel to do with this divine gift? Was he to utter prophecies, to sing psalms, to write laws? Not at all. He was " to devise cunning works, to work in gold and in silver and in brass, and in cutting of stones to set them, and in carving of timber; to work in all manner of workmanship." It is possible, then, that God's thought may express itself in cunning works in wood or iron. It did so express itself in the olden time, and why not now? True, the building on which this man Bezaleel was thus divinely qualified to work was the tabernacle; but do you not think that God needs inspired workmen in building the grander temple of modern civilization? and do you not suppose that now, as in the olden time, those who fashion this grand structure are working under his guidance?

It is not then, working-men, a careless Providence, or a malevolent Providence, that fills your workshops with these facile instruments of labor. The selfishness of men may have had much to do with producing them; but the selfishness of men is made in this matter as in others to praise God, and to further the designs of an infinite benevolence. And I should like to show you, if I can, how these machines, which seem on a narrow view to be your enemies, are really working not only for the good of the world as a whole, but for your good.

It was no wonder, at the outset, that men who had had no wide range of observation, and who were unfamiliar with the laws of political economy, should fail to understand that labor-saving machines help the laborer. The obvious fact was that there was a machine that did the work of two or perhaps of ten men: was it not certain, that, if the machine were allowed to work, it would throw the one or the nine, not required to operate it, out of employment? That was the apparent consequence; but it must at length begin to appear, even to ignorant men, that a great many elements have to be taken into the account in solving such a problem as this. Other results arise from the employment of such machinery, which are not so apparent, at first sight, and which are yet very important to the working-man.

In the first place, machinery tends to cheapen the commodities that working-men must buy. The prices of nearly all the articles consumed by the laborer are greatly reduced by the use of machinery.

Moreover, the machines, by lowering the price of the commodities they produce, tend powerfully to increase the demand for these commodities, and greatly to stimulate production.

Take, for example, the trade with which I am most

familiar, — printing. When the machine-press was introduced, it naturally appeared to the printers that some of them would lose their employment by reason of it; but what has been the result? The improved facilities for printing have so increased the demand for printed matter, by cheapening it, and putting it within the reach of a larger number of readers, that now, with the machines in use, many more persons are employed at printing than formerly, — a greater number, I think, in proportion to the whole population. The work is lighter, and the wages are better.

The same thing is true of every other mechanical trade. I do not think it is possible to mention any branch of production in which the use of labor-saving machinery has not increased instead of diminishing the number of laborers, and raised instead of reducing the wages of labor. Since I was a farmer's boy, twenty years ago, a great deal of farm machinery has come into general use: farm-work is much lighter than it used to be, and the wages paid to laborers are much higher than they used to be; not only positively but relatively higher. The average price of a day's labor on the farm will buy more of the necessaries of life to-day than it would twenty years ago.

It is true that the gains which have come to workmen through the introduction of machinery have been slow. They have not kept pace with the increase of wealth; nor will they, until the machines are owned, as well as operated, by the workmen. Nevertheless machinery has already brought a positive pecuniary advantage to the laboring classes; and, under a better organization of labor, it is destined to secure to them far greater benefits.

There is one other result of the introduction of machinery to which I wish to allude; that is the intellectual improvement of workmen. It takes more intelligence to operate a machine than it does to handle a tool. There are principles involved in the construction of the machine which the operator must understand more or less clearly or he cannot manage it. It is true that some men work all their lives with machinery without acquiring any very satisfactory knowledge of the principles on which it is constructed: nevertheless some ideas are picked up by the dullest; and the general result is a considerable increase of the knowledge, and a corresponding development of the mental powers, of the workmen.

For this reason machinery was introduced into the South to a very limited extent before the destruction of slavery. It would have been difficult, no doubt, to teach the slaves to use machinery; but it was not so much the difficulty as the danger of the undertaking that kept the masters from it. It would not have been easy to initiate Sambo into the mysteries of the mowing-machine or the power-loom; but he would have comprehended them at length, and along with them several other things that it was not safe for him to know. You cannot keep men in servitude who work with machinery. The intelligence that suffices for such work is an intelligence that will forge its own weapons of deliverance from bondage. As Prof. Cairnes of London clearly pointed out in his masterly work on the causes of the late war in this country, the only hope of keeping the blacks in subjection lay in the policy of the masters, — a policy in most cases instinctively rather than deliberately chosen, — of keeping them employed with the rudest kind of tools, in doing the roughest sort of work.

While it is true that any kind of work is better for the mind than idleness, it is also true that the work which demands the most skill and thought is the work which most rapidly develops the mind; and hence the improvement of implements and machinery is one powerful means not only of ameliorating the physical condition of the laboring man, but also of cultivating his intellect. It is thought that educates, — the contact with quick and fertile mind; and it matters not whether this contact be produced by a voice or a book or a machine: the result is the same.

I am looking for the time, — though doubtless I

shall never see it, — when the forces of nature shall be so broken to the will of man that the necessaries of life will be easily gained, and along with them such abundant instruction in the true methods of living, such ample light in the ways in which workmen now walk darkly, that want and strife will be almost unknown. By and by the world will be not only the storehouse of an unfailing bounty, and the temple of a pure religion, but the school of a divine wisdom to all mankind. While, therefore, I do not despise manual labor, I look to see its burdens lightened every year, and hope for the time when the benumbing toils that now dull the faculties of so many millions shall give place to a freer life, to labors less painful, to activities that shall be full of zest for the workman.

This state of things, when it comes, will be in no small measure the direct result of the introduction of those machines for the increase of production and the relief of labor of which I have sometimes heard my friends among the working-men bitterly complain. These complaints were not unnatural ; but perhaps a careful examination of the whole subject will enable us to see that they are most unwise. That Divine Providence under whose eye all these industrial revolutions are going on, cares for the working-man as much as for the capitalist. Christ

himself was a carpenter's son, was he not? Do
you think that God forgets you? Do you believe
that that "increasing purpose" of his which "runs
through all the ages," widening the thoughts of men
and lifting up their lives, leaves you out altogether?
No, my friends, that cannot be. The forces of the
world, in their full scope, are working to your good.
And if you will quietly sit down and count not only
the hardships of your lot, but your advantages and
your gains, I believe that you will find it so.

But leaving aside these larger results for which
we look in the future, and these hopeful assurances
which we draw from the Christian religion itself
concerning the lot of the working-man, is there con-
veyed in that religion any truth that touches the
present life and the daily labor of our working
people? Has Christianity any thing to say about
work and how to do it?

It would be strange if it had not. Christ was not
only known to men as the carpenter's son; he was
himself a carpenter. Doubtless he learned the trade
of his reputed father, and worked at it till he was
thirty years old. Of his chosen apostles, several
were fishermen; nearly all of them, probably, were
workmen in some humble calling. There is a little
doubt about Judas. Of his antecedents we know
absolutely nothing; it would seem, however, that his

training must have been that of a financier, rather
than that of a laborer. But since the Founder of
Christianity, and most of its first teachers, belonged
without doubt to the working classes, we should
naturally expect that it would have something to say
about the duties of working people. We are not
disappointed in this expectation. The utterances of
the New Testament on this subject are not, it is true,
very radical when compared with the modern type
of radicalism; no attempt is made to disturb the
rights of property, or to array the different classes in
society against each other. In all such conflicts as
these Christ declined to have any part. Once, when
a man came to him and said, "Master, speak to my
brother that he divide the inheritance with me," he
answered sternly, "Man, who made me a judge or a
divider over you?" And then, turning to those
round about him, he said, "Take heed and beware
of covetousness, for a man's life consisteth not in the
abundance of the things which he possesseth." When
any quarrel was going on about positions or possessions, Christ took part with neither side; he would
not give his countenance to any scheme for settling
by force or by law the relations between hostile
classes: what he struck at was that spirit of covetousness which is the root of every such disagreement,
which makes the employer extortionate and rapa-

cious, and the workman indolent and greedy. When that is once exterminated from the hearts of men there will be no more strife between capital and labor; and to exterminate it was the work that Christ came to do.

Nevertheless the duties of working-men are referred to incidentally more than once in the New Testament. I shall mention but one such passage. The words are from the pen of St. Paul, who, though a man of fine education and large experience of the world, was a practical mechanic. His home was in Cilicia, a province of Asia Minor, which was famous in those days for its manufactures of hair-cloth, the substance of which tents are made. He was a tent-maker by trade; and the New Testament tells us that, when he was on his missionary tours, he sometimes supported himself by working at his trade rather than "be chargeable to any" of those to whom he was preaching. Paul knew, therefore, something of the questions in which working-men are interested; and he has something to say to them in nearly all of his epistles. In his letter to the Christians at Colosse, he addresses various classes of persons, and gives them counsel about their daily lives, "Whatsoever ye do, do it heartily, as unto the Lord and not unto men." These words. are addressed to servants, and the servants to whom they are addressed were slaves.

And Paul counsels them to do their work heartily.
If such counsel is good for a slave, how much better
is it for a freeman! If a slave ought to put his soul
into his work, — for this is what Paul's expression
means, — how much more should a freeman!

" Whatsoever ye do, do it from the soul," says the
great apostle to the Colossian slaves. This means a
little more than that it should be done willingly.
The soul is the man : it is the intelligence and the
conscience, as well as the affections. And Paul
seems to mean that men who are called to any work
ought to do it intelligently and conscientiously as
well as cheerfully.

Intelligently, I say. There is room for the exercise of intelligence in every avocation.

" Pray, how do you mix your colors? " queried the
young painter of the old artist. " With brains, sir,"
was the short but sufficient answer. There is no
product of our hands with which brains may not be
profitably mixed. Give your mind to your calling.

All work is art. There are artists in dirt, at whose
feet I would fain sit in these days of garden-making ;
rude men, who with shovel and rake will slope a
bank or trace a winding walk in a manner wholly
beyond my power of imitation. There are artists in
dry goods: look at the pictures they make for you in
the show-windows! There are artists in wood,

whom men commonly call carpenters; and artists in iron, generally known as blacksmiths, — men whose handiwork is always shapely, symmetrical, beautiful. There are artists in household work; indeed, the very finest and most delicate art is all the while displaying itself in the arrangement and adornment of our houses. In short, there is an ideal perfection which ought to be striven after in our mechanical and domestic labor as really as in what are called the fine arts. God has made every thing beautiful in its time. I suppose that he takes pleasure in his handiwork, not only because of its fitness, but because of its beauty. Is there any reason why you should not take pleasure in your handiwork for the same reason?

Conscience, too, ought to be put into work. This world would be a great deal better world to live in than it is, if a little more conscience were put into our carpentry and our mason-work and our plumbing and our cabinet-making and our upholstering and our tailoring and our shoe-making; if some of our painters that do not call themselves artists mixed their paints with conscience as well as with brains. A vast amount of bad work is done in these days, — slovenly work, dishonest work. That is one way in which the moral sense of the people is blunted and depraved. Lies and shams are all around us; and we become so accustomed to them that truth and integrity sometimes seem to be quite out of place in this world. "Things are not what they seem," says the poet. No, I shouldn't think they were. Almost nothing that man has made is what it seems. Under a fair outside, beneath a thick coat of varnish, all sorts of falsehoods are hiding.

Now, I wish you could be made to see that work of this sort is morally wrong. A lie that is expressed in wood is no better than a lie that is expressed in words. Dishonest work is just as bad as dishonest talk. You ought not to be guilty of it. It may be that you are in the employ of those who require you to work in this way. If they do, I suppose the fault is theirs and not yours. But do keep it before your thought that all such work is really immoral, and that the millennium will never come till the world is rid of it.

Sometimes you are eager to discover ways of doing good. Begin right here, then. Do your work well. You can add very greatly to the sum of the world's happiness by doing honest work. Of how much discomfort, and bad temper, and other sin your bad work is the cause, none of you are perhaps fully aware.

But what reason does this apostle urge why these servants should put their souls into their work; why they should do it intelligently, conscientiously, heartily? It is that all their work is done in the sight of God. "As unto the Lord and not unto men, you labor," says Paul. "It is not for your earthly master's sake, it is not for your own sake, that I urge it: it is for the Lord's sake." To the Ephesian servants he gives like counsel: "With good-will doing service, as to the Lord and not to men; knowing that, whatsoever good thing any man doeth, the same shall he receive of the Lord, whether he be bond or free."

Paul is not talking here about religious or charitable work at all. He is talking about the kind of work at which these slaves were kept by their masters. "Whatsoever good thing any man doeth," then, — whatsoever good carpentry, whatsoever good tent-making, whatsoever good gardening, whatsoever good house-serving, — the Lord will watch and reward. If he be a bondsman, and get for his pains nothing but kicks and buffetings from his master, let him be patient, and remember that the great Artificer on high, all whose work is good, and who delights in all good work, is noting his faithfulness and thoroughness, and will recompense him for it in due season. If he be working for wages, and all the credit of his good work go to the master-workman, no matter: there is one reckoning in which no man will be cheated of any credit that belongs to him.

In short, my friends, never forget that there are right ways and wrong ways of doing your work; that the right way is God's way; that you may honor and please him, not only by a faithful discharge of the duties you have engaged to perform for men, but also by a careful and painstaking performance of the work itself.

## II.

## LABOR AND CAPITAL.

HISTORY shows us three different systems by which
capital and labor have been brought together, — the
system of slavery, the wages system, and the system
of co-operation.

In the first of these there is no conflict between
capital and labor, because the capitalist owns the
laborer. On the one side is force, on the other side
submission. Labor and capital are indeed identified,
because the laborer is part of the property of the
capitalist which is engaged in production. There is
no dispute about wages ; the word is never heard.

This system of slavery is recognized and regulated
in the legislation of the Bible, just as polygamy and
blood vengeance are recognized and regulated. The
laws of Moses do not sanction either of these evils :

they only set bounds to them, and secure their administration on certain principles of justice and humanity
which will in due time put an end to them. And
when these principles begin to root themselves in the
convictions of the people, prophets arise announcing
the higher law of perfect righteousness, of which
the Levitical legislation was only the precursor; and
bidding the people, in the name of the Lord, to
undo the heavy burdens, and to let the oppressed
go free.

Under such a moral regimen, slavery could not
thrive. And when Christ appeared, declaring that
the law and the prophets were all summed up in the
rule which bids us do to others as we would have
others do to us, the doom of the system was sealed.
There is no express legislation against it in the New
Testament; but there is no great need of express
legislation against wearing fur overcoats in July.
What Christianity did was to create a moral atmosphere in which slavery could not exist.

Men have always been quoting the Bible on the
side of slavery; but, while pettifogging theologians
have been searching its pages for texts with which
to prop their system, the spirit of the book has been
steadily undermining the system.

There are those who still choose to represent Christianity as the ally of despotism. A newspaper pub-

lished in this Commonwealth made, not long ago, the
sweeping assertion, that " freedom and Christianity
are fundamentally and irreconcilably antagonistic;
and that whoever strikes a blow for the one strikes a
blow against the other." In contradiction to this
statement, we may quote the whole of history. Go
back to the dark ages, to the period when the
Church was most corrupt and faithless, and you
will find that even then it always was the champion
of the oppressed. Mr. Fitzjames Stephen, one of
the most brilliant of living English writers, — himself a barrister and a student of ancient law, though
a sceptic as regards revealed religion, — bears
this testimony to what Christianity has done for liberty : —

" The glory of the mediæval Church is the resistance which it
offered to tyranny of every kind.  The typical bishop of those times
is always upholding a righteous cause against kings and emperors, or
exhorting masters to let their slaves go free, or giving sanctuary to
harassed fugitives. . . . What is true of the bishops is true in a still
more eminent degree of the religious orders."

Read Guizot's History of Civilization in Europe
for abundant confirmation of these statements. The
power of the keys which the Church put into the
hands of the priest was used in behalf of the enslaved,
in unlocking their shackles and in lightening their

burdens. The destruction of the feudal system in Europe, and the abolition of serfdom, was, in considerable part, the work of the Christian Church.

I have dwelt upon this fact of history, because I wish to make it plain to working-men that the religion of Christ is not hostile to their interests; that it has indeed done more for the mitigation of their hardships, and the enlargement of their privileges, than any other power on earth. The suspicion with which the laboring classes, especially in Europe, have been taught by some of their leaders to regard Christianity, may be excusable in view of the corrupt and perverted nature of the Christianity by which they are surrounded; but it would surely be impossible, if they had any clear notion of what the religion of Christ is, and of what it has done for them.

If, then, this first system in which history brings together the capitalist and the laborer, the system of bondage, be largely a thing of the past; if the workman has now, in many lands, been emancipated, — this result is due, in great part, to the prevalence of the Christian religion.

The second of these systems is that in which, throughout the civilized world, we now find capital and labor, in which they freely exchange services. The workman gives his work in exchange for the employer's money. There is a contract between

them, by which the rate of remuneration is fixed.
The fundamental principle of this wages system is
competition, that is, conflict.  If all men were benevolent, if the Golden Rule were the rule of all
exchanges, of course this need not be; but unfortunately, the business of the world is for the most
part organized on a basis of self-interest; and thus,
by the wages system, the interest of the employer
and the interest of the laborer come directly into
collision.  The laborer wants to get all he can for his
labor, the employer wants to give for it no more
than he must; and between the two there is an
unceasing struggle for advantage and mastery.
How sharp and fierce this struggle is, let the history
of England and America for the last twenty-five
years bear record.

Thus the second stage in the progress of labor is
a stage of conflict.  Slavery first, then war.  All the
kingdoms of the world's industry are now in a state
of war.  Sometimes the strife is suppressed, and
there is apparent peace; sometimes the warfare is
only one of words or of unfriendly combinations: but
very often, as lately in the Pennsylvania coal-fields,
the parties come to blows.  Violence is constantly
resorted to when the contest waxes hot.  Either
between the employers and the laborers there is a
direct issue of force, or else part of the laborers

take the side of the employers, and are attacked as traitors to the army of labor. But even when the arbitrament of brickbats and bludgeons is not appealed to, there is none the less a state of war. Capital will assert and maintain its claims, so will labor; and neither will yield to the other more than it is compelled to do. Labor and capital work together in production. They must work together. Capital is worth nothing without labor; labor cannot subsist without capital. The contest arises in dividing the profits of this joint production. Over these profits there is a perpetual quarrel. It is generally believed, among working-men, that the capitalist gets the lion's share of them; it is commonly asserted nowadays by capitalists, that business cannot be done without a loss on account of the high rate of wages. I do not pretend to know which side is right: I only see the quarrel going on, and wish that it might in some way be stopped. Can it be stopped? That is the question.

I have read what the political economists have to say about this matter, and I confess that it does not help me very much. There is much learned talk about the wages fund; and no little dispute among the professors as to what this wages fund is, and whether the laborers are paid out of it or out of the product. Indeed, it would seem that the warfare of which the wages system is the occasion is not confined to the factories, but extends to the universities as well. They tell us that a certain part of the profits of production is set aside by the capitalists to pay future laborers, and that the price of wages depends upon the relation of this wages fund to the number of laborers, and can depend on nothing else; that when the wages fund is large, and the laborers are few, the wages will be high because each man's share will be larger; that, on the other hand, when the wages fund is small and the laborers are many, the wages must be low because each man's share will be small. Accordingly, they tell us, the whole question is one of supply and demand: the rate of wages is determined by fixed economical laws; the will of the employer cannot alter it; no combinations of workmen can affect it; it is just as vain to undertake to control it by legislation or by organization as it would be to control the winds or the tides in that way.

Well, that may be true, and probably is true if men are not moral beings; if the doctrines of materialism or of high Calvinism are true, and if the actions of men are determined by forces outside of themselves. But we shall venture to assume for a little while longer that the wills of men are free; that their choices have something to do with their destinies; and that by the presentation to them of truth, by an appeal to their reason and their moral sense, their conduct may be influenced. The questions of social science or of political economy are in part moral questions; and my business is to find out what are the moral considerations that enter into this problem, by which the strife between labor and capital may be tempered, and the good of both parties may be promoted.

In the first place, then, it would appear that what the economists call the wages fund — that portion of the capital which is devoted to the remuneration of labor — does depend somewhat on the will of the capitalist. It depends partly on his habits of living whether it shall be increased or diminished. If he is lavish in his personal expenditures, he will not of course have so large a wages fund as if he is economical. Here is an employer who during the year spends ten thousand dollars in the merest luxuries of life, — in feasting and in dressing, — in that which is consumed and cast aside with the using: must not his power to remunerate his workmen be reduced by that amount? Might he not, if he had chosen, have used this money in increasing the wages of his laborers?

"But that is all nonsense," answers the capitalist. "Business is business. Supply and demand, my dear

parson! Supply and demand! Every man must
pay the market price for labor, and any man is a
fool who pays more." No, my friend : you do yourself wrong. You are not wholly the victim of these
economical laws : you resist them and rule them
sometimes, in the interest of humanity. There is a
poor man in your employ who has been partly
disabled. In the market, he could get almost nothing for his labor. But you take pity on him and his
household, and continue his wages at the rate you
paid him when he was in health. That is not
" supply and demand " at all. Another law comes
in here, a better law, — the law of love. You do
bring it in, now and then, to alleviate the hardships
that would result from the inflexible enforcement of
those economical laws of which you speak. The
question is, whether you might not bring it in a little
oftener ; whether, indeed, you might not incorporate
it into all your dealings with your working-men ; and
instead of saying, "Business is business," say, "Business is stewardship: business is the high calling
of God, into which I am bound to put conscience
and benevolence, as well as sagacity and enterprise."
This is just what Christian principle ought to effect
on the side of capital, in the relation between
capital and labor ; just what it does effect in some
degree : but if, on the present basis of production,

there is to be any enduring peace between these now warring parties, there must be on the part of capitalists a good deal more of this intervention of Christian principle, to hold in check the cruel tendencies of the economic forces.

Not only on the side of the capitalist must this spirit of sweet reasonableness find expression: the workman must govern himself by the same law. If employers are sometimes heartless and extortionate, laborers are sometimes greedy and headstrong. I have known of more than one case in which workmen have demanded an increase of wages when the business was yielding no profits; when the balance every month was on the wrong side of the employer's books; when with the strictest economy in his personal expenditures, and the most careful attention to his affairs, he was growing poorer instead of richer every day. I have known other cases, in which workmen have resisted a reduction of wages, when that was the only condition on which the business could be carried on without disaster. As a mere matter of policy, this is suicidal. For workmen to exact a rate of pay that shall destroy the business by which they get their living, is simply to kill the goose that lays the golden egg every day, because she does not lay two every day. It is not, however, with the policy of the transaction that I am chiefly

concerned, but with the rightfulness of it.  Grave
wrongs are often in this way inflicted upon employers: their business is paralyzed, their credit is
impaired, their property is swept away; and, in the
destruction of the enterprises which they are carrying on, their power to help and serve their fellow-
men is crippled.  For nothing is plainer than that a
man who organizes and carries on any honest business, in which he gives employment and fair remuneration to laborers, ought to be considered a public
benefactor.  All depends, of course, upon the
manner in which he manages his business.  If it is
managed in the spirit of Shylock, it may be an injury
to the community; but if it is based upon principles
of justice and fair play, it is a benefit to the community, and the destruction of it is a calamity and a
wrong, not only to him, but also to the public.
Any combination of laborers that undertakes to
cripple or to kill an enterprise of this kind is engaged in a bad business.

"Is this meant, then, for a condemnation of
strikes?" asks somebody.  Not necessarily.  I have
no doubt that such combinations of laborers are
often unwise and unprofitable; that, as a general
thing, they result in more loss than gain to the
laboring classes; but it does not appear to me that
they are always morally wrong.  This is a free coun-

try : if you do not choose to work for a man unless he will pay you a certain rate of wages, no one can compel you to do so; and if ten or twenty or two hundred of your fellow-workmen are of the same mind, and prefer to be idle for a season rather than to take less than the price demanded for their services, they have a right to do it. But it seems to me that you ought to consider whether by your combination you may not be inflicting serious damage upon the whole community, and that you ought to have some regard to the public good in what you do. If the Christian law governs your conduct, you will think of this. But if you can satisfy yourself that the public welfare will take no serious detriment from your action, I do not know that it can be shown to be morally wrong. You and your fellows may find it for your advantage to take this course ; and it is a lawful means of securing your own advantage. On the other hand, it may be for your disadvantage ; you may be worse off in the end : but that is your concern and the concern of those dependent on you. So long as you pay your honest debts, and support your families, no one else has a right to complain if you do take a course which results in loss and damage to yourself.

Certain measures are, however, frequently resorted to at such times that are morally wrong.

4*

You have a right to refuse to work for less than a
certain rate, and you have a right to *influence* others
to join with you in this refusal; but you have no
right to use force or intimidation to keep any man
from working for less. Nobody has any right to
force you to work: you have no right to compel
anybody to be idle who is satisfied with less wages
than you demand. He may be a poor workman; but
that is his employer's concern, not yours. If you
can persuade him to join you, very good; but you
have no right to lay a straw in his way if he refuses
to join you. We believe in free labor in this country, do we not? And that belief implies that no
laborer ought to be enslaved or coerced by his employer or by his fellow-laborers.

If, now, workmen will endeavor to deal with their
employers and with one another without threatening
or violence, in a spirit of good-will and fair play;
recognizing the important service that is rendered
them by the men who organize the various industries
by which they get a living, and trying to render a
fair equivalent in work for the wages they receive;
they will do *their* part toward terminating this unhappy strife which has so long prevailed between
labor and capital. It is a most melancholy quarrel:
society is disturbed and unsettled by it, and the
human brotherhood is rent into discordant and hos-

tile factions. If the capitalist would measure his profits, and the working-man his wages, by the Golden Rule, there would be instant peace. And that is the only way to secure peace on the basis of the wages system. Political economy cannot secure it: its maxims breed more strife than they allay. Political economy only deals with natural forces; and the natural forces, even those which manifest themselves in society, often seem to be heartless and cruel. The law of nature would appear to be the survival of the strongest; and it is the workings of this law with which political economy has to do. Legislation cannot stop this strife. What, indeed, is law but an edict of force? Behind every law is the policeman's billy or the soldier's bayonet. It has no meaning, no efficacy, unless there is force behind it. And you cannot make peace with a sword between these contending interests. A gentler influence, a subtler but a mightier force, must take possession of the minds and hearts of the combatants on either side before the warfare will cease. If the spirit that dwelt in Christ be in you, — if you will learn to "look not every man on his own things, but also on the things of others;" to love your neighbors as yourselves; to put yourselves in their places now and then, and judge their conduct and yours too from their point of view, — you will speedily come

to terms in all your quarrels. And is it not about
time for all of you, capitalists and laborers, in view
of the wasting warfare that you have so long been
waging, to lay to heart the injunction of Paul, " If
ye bite and devour one another, take heed that ye
be not consumed one of another " ?

I must own that I have not much hope, however,
that the war to which the wages system gives
occasion will ever cease until the system is abolished
or greatly modified. Christian principle can do
much to mitigate the strife, so far as it gains control
of the lives of men; but it will be a good while
before the masses of men, whether capitalists or
laborers, are so fully governed by the Christian
law that they will cease to struggle for the advantage and mastery. The wages system is better than
slavery, because conflict is better than apathy; but
there is something better than the wages system, and
I hope that we some time shall reach it.

The subjugation of labor by capital is the first
stage in the progress of industry; the second stage
is the warfare between labor and capital; the third
is the identification of labor and capital by some
application of the principle of co-operation. This is
what we are coming to by and by. The long struggle between these two conflicting interests promises

to end by uniting them, and making the laborer his own capitalist.

I need not stop to describe this system to you : you are all familiar with the principles on which it rests. By combining their savings, the workmen employ themselves, and divide the profits of the business among themselves.

Not only will peace be promoted by such an organization of labor, but thrift and morality also. None but those who have a mind to save their earnings can become members of such an association. Business requires capital, and the capital must be provided from the savings of the workmen themselves. In furnishing a strong motive to economy, co-operation will do good. The miseries of the working people in this country are often due to extravagance and improvidence, rather than to insufficient incomes. Besides, it is always necessary in these associations to enforce rigid rules of moral conduct. Drunkards or idlers are immediately turned out. Sober and steady workers are not at all disposed to divide their profits with the lazy and dissolute.

We may hope, too, that co-operation will secure greater economy of material, and better work. The workmen working for themselves, and having a direct interest in the profits of their work, are likely to be careful about waste. This carefulness will be of advantage not only to them, but to everybody else. The world is enriched not only by the discovery of new wealth, but by the frugal use of that which is already in men's hands. All waste makes the world poorer.

For the same reason, because each man is working for himself, it is directly for his interest to make all his work as nearly perfect as he can; and that is a result at which the whole world ought to rejoice.

Such are some of the results which may be expected from the success of industrial co-operation. The expectation is not based upon theory, but upon accomplished facts. Already in France and in England the experiment has been tried with remarkable success. A year ago, Mr. Thomas Brassey, M.P., in an address before the Co-operative Congress, stated that there were in England and Wales 746 co-operative societies, with more than 300,000 members, the share capital amounting to nearly $14,000,000; and that during the previous year they had transacted a business amounting to nearly $57,000,000. The larger part of this business, however, was in the mercantile rather than in the manufacturing line. In England the system has worked better in distribution than in production; but there has been considerable success in both directions.

But some of you may ask why a system so excellent has not been universally adopted. There are two or three reasons. So far as this country is concerned, the wages of labor have hitherto been so large that working-men have been pretty well satisfied with their condition, and have not been driven to devise new ways of gaining a livelihood.

In the second place, working-men everywhere lack confidence in the honesty and fidelity of one another. They hesitate to risk their savings in such enterprises, for fear some faithless treasurer will default and run away with them. Very many of the co-operative stores in this country have come to grief in this way.

In the third place, in the members of such an organization, a certain trait is essential which I may find it difficult to describe in one word, and which is not so fully developed as it might be among our working-people, or among our people who do not work, for that matter. It is the trait that makes a man work well in harness. It is the spirit of concession, the spirit of subordination, the spirit that thinks less of personal power or gain or glory than of the common good. It is the spirit that we ought to find as the bond of union in all our churches, and *do* find sometimes, thank God! It is the virtue Paul inculcates when he bids the Romans, " Be kindly affectioned one toward another with brotherly love, in honor preferring one another." Where this spirit abounds, there is always unity and fruitfulness; where this spirit is not, there is confusion and all kinds of evil. And it is the absence of this spirit that hinders the success of many of our co-operative societies.

There is or was an Iron-Workers' Co-operative Association in Troy, N.Y., whose success at the beginning was quite remarkable. Last summer I wrote to a gentleman living there, to inquire how it was flourishing; and he replied that it seemed to be losing ground. Dissensions among the members were killing it. There had been frequent changes of managers, and it appeared that every man wanted to be boss.

More than one association of the kind has met its fate in this way. You cannot have co-operation till you can find men who can co-operate. How can you ?

Add to these considerations, the fact that comparatively few among our working-men have the intelligence and sagacity requisite to organize and manage a large business, and you have a pretty clear explanation of the reasons why co-operation has not been more generally introduced. Before the production of the country can be carried on in this way, there must be a great improvement in the mental and moral qualities of working-people. But this improvement is steadily going on; our free schools and our open churches are offering to the children of our mechanics and operatives a culture in morality and intelligence that we may hope will qualify them after a while, to take their destinies into their own hands. The hour is not yet come, but it is sure to come; and the bell that strikes it will

" Ring out the feud of rich and poor."

The transition from the wages system to the system of co-operation is likely to be made through the introduction of what are called industrial partnerships : by which the work-people in a manufacturing establishment are given an interest in the business; and, in addition to their wages, a stipulated portion of the profits is divided among them at the close of every year, in proportion to the amount of their earnings. It would seem that the times are fully ripe for the adoption of this principle. I have no doubt that many of our manufacturers would find it greatly to their advantage to introduce it; that it would result in securing steadier workmen and better work, and that it would put an end to strikes and all other forms of strife.

But, if I am right, working-men, as to the obsta-

4

cles that hinder your entrance upon the better system, they are mainly such as arise out of your own
defective conduct toward each other; they are such,
too, as the Christian religion is calculated to remove.
Indeed, is it not just because the Christian principle
does not govern your lives, that you cannot co-operate? If the law of love ruled your treatment of
each other, you would have no difficulty whatever in
working together; in taking into your own hands all
the grand industrial enterprises of the age, and carrying them forward with a vigor and a success that the
world has never seen under the principle of competition.

For, let no one fail to see that co-operation is nothing more than the arrangement of the essential
factors of industry according to the Christian rule,
"We being many are one body in Christ, and every
one members one of another." It is capital and
labor adjusting themselves to the form of Christianity; and, like every other outward symbol, is a false
deceitful show, a dead form, unless filled with the
living spirit of Christianity itself.

Working-men, I ask you to ponder these things.
There are those who seek to make you think that the
Church of Christ is an enemy, or at best but a heartless stepmother, greedy to get your service, but
careless of your welfare. I know that there are

elements in the Church — corrupted fragments of the Church — against which such a charge as this might be truly brought; but it is not true of the Christian doctrine or the Christian system. The power that has stricken the shackles from the laborer, that has lightened his burdens, that has lifted him up to a happier and a nobler life, and that has put into his hands the key of a great future, is the power that came into the world when Christ was born.

## III.

## HARD TIMES AND HOW TO EASE THEM.

IF what everybody says be true, it must be that the times are hard upon which we have fallen. The merchants, the capitalists, the employing classes, the professional people, are all complaining about them; everywhere they are the staple of conversation. There is no famine, nor any thing like it. The necessaries of life are abundant, and not very dear. Absolute want is scarcely known among us: most of our people get enough to eat, and something to wear, and something to warm themselves withal; but a great many of them fail to get as much as they would like of the comforts of life, if not of its absolute necessaries.

As for the capitalists, no doubt they have encountered, during the last two or three years, a great shrinkage of values, — of estimated values, at any rate. Many have suffered real losses; but many more have suffered speculative losses. Some are not so rich as they were; hardly anybody is so rich as he thought he was. Many who supposed that they had accumulated enough to live upon without labor find their funds or their real estate depreciated, so that they must set themselves to eke out their income by their earnings. Business that was very profitable a few years ago is much less profitable now; some enterprises are carried on at a steady loss, in hope of the better times which seem to come but tardily.

As for the working-people, not many of them had any thing to lose; but their work is not so steady as they could wish, and their wages have been reduced, so that their annual earnings are perceptibly smaller than they were two or three years ago.

Of all this stagnation of trade, this paralysis of industry, there must be causes. Is it not worth while to look for them? Would it be amiss if some prophet of the Lord should bid us, as Haggai once bade the people of Judæa when harder times were prevailing among them, to consider our ways, — the ways by which we have come into this distress; the ways in which we are stumbling along now, in a discouraged endeavor to get out of it?

5*

The real losses that this country has suffered, and
that have had their part in producing these hard
times, are not far to seek.  Within the past fifteen
years, an enormous amount of property has been
destroyed in this country.  The waste of the war
was simply prodigious.  Hundreds of millions of
wealth were obliterated utterly ; burnt up, demol-
ished, shot away in iron and lead and gunpowder.
Of course, such a destruction of property must im-
poverish the land.  A nation may tide over the
shoal of debt, heaped up in such a time, on a flood
of paper money ; but the due-bills of the government must be settled by and by, and when that time
comes it will be seen that paper is poor stuff with
which to patch up the breaches that war has made
in the national capital.  Vast regions of the South
were devastated by the war ; and since that war the
people of those regions have been unable to make
any large contribution to the national wealth.  They
cannot buy of us the fabrics with which we were
wont to supply them, because they have nothing
wherewith to pay for them.  That stops our mill-
wheels, while the taxes that have followed in the
wake of the war reduce our incomes and burden
our industries.

This is the inevitable result of a severe and destructive war.  If a nation chooses to dance to the

music of the musket, it must be ready, when the
piping times of peace come, to pay the piper.
Whatsoever a nation soweth, that shall it also reap.
If it sows destruction, it will reap poverty. There
is no discharge in any war from the burdens that the
war brings after it.

I do not mean to say that the nation was not justified, when the issue was raised, in meeting it just as
it did; the nation is worth all that it has cost to
save it, and more : but it may be well for us to remember that the whole land was to blame for the
state of things that resulted in the war, and that we
are only reaping now what we have sown. Such a
moral enormity, such an economical folly as slavery
was, must bring calamity in due season upon the
nation that suffered it. Yet we at the North did
suffer it; we were not at all in earnest about putting
an end to it; we resisted for years all efforts to set
bounds to it, and secure its peaceful extinction. We
wanted Southern trade more than we wanted justice
and righteousness. Our subservience to the slave-
power emboldened it to push its exactions more and
more imperiously, till at length we were forced to
face the bitter alternative of disunion or war.
Twenty-five years of truckling was what did it.
And we are paying the penalty of that to-day. We
paid its first instalments in five years of carnage;

but there was gold as well as blood in the bond, and the bond is not yet quite discharged.

The two classes at the North that were most unwilling to have the demands of slavery challenged were the commercial class and the laboring class. The first did not want to lose their customers; the others were afraid that, if the slaves were emancipated, there would be an irruption of negro labor into the industries of the North. These two classes are suffering most to-day from the results of the war. It may be well for us all to read in this chapter of history the lesson that the way of righteousness is always the safest road in the end.

Since the waste of the war came to an end, we have suffered several severe losses by fire. Two of our most flourishing cities and several smaller towns have been almost wiped out in this way. And the fact must not be overlooked, that property destroyed by fire is totally destroyed. The insurance brings some relief to the individual sufferer, but it makes the community no richer. The two or three hundred millions of wealth that were consumed by the great fires in Boston and Chicago made the whole nation so much the poorer. All over the country the incomes of men were reduced by this destruction; and the final effect has been to depress trade and cripple industry. This too is a penalty which we are paying for our carelessness and flimsiness in building. If you sow tinder-boxes in your city streets, you shall reap conflagrations.

Another cause of the hard times is the waste of which the whole people are guilty. The materials of living are used by Americans with a most lavish prodigality. Mr. McCulloch, writing from Europe only a short time since about the unthriftiness of our countrymen, expressed the opinion that the people of France would live sumptuously every day on what is wasted every day by the people of America. How to make the most of what he has, is a lesson that hardly anybody in this country has learned. If the science of domestic economy were as fully understood by Americans as it is by Frenchmen, there would be much less talk here of hard times.

Not only by a careless use of the necessaries of life, but also by a reckless consumption of that which is at once unnecessary and pernicious, the land is impoverished. From the National Bureau of Statistics we learn that six hundred millions of dollars are annually expended in America for intoxicating liquors. This sum exceeds by more than one hundred millions of dollars the combined gross earnings of all the railroads in the United States. The rum bills of the nation are as large as its meat bills. Even were we to say nothing about the moral mischiefs that result from the use of intoxicants, this waste of wealth to which they lead is something appalling. And any analysis of the causes of our hard times, that left this out of the account, would be altogether incomplete.

Close akin to waste is extravagance. The one is a positive, the other a relative term. He is extravagant whose rate of living is in excess of his income. No matter how small his income is, if it is sufficient to support life, he is extravagant if he lives beyond it, if he suffers his great expectations of future gains to influence his present expenditures. And that is what many of us have been doing. The sudden gains that came through the inflation of our currency completely turned the heads of hundreds of thousands of our people, and led them to adopt a scale of living which it was quite beyond their power to maintain. This general fact has been well illustrated in our own neighborhood. Sober Connecticut Valley farmers, living prudently and well on their yearly productions, suddenly found themselves in possession of greatly increased incomes, derived from the cultivation of tobacco. The effect of this was to raise their ideas of life enormously. Their wants multiplied much faster than their wealth. So intoxicated were they with the prospects before them, that they began to spend not only all they got for their crops, but to mortgage future crops for luxuries. Fine houses, palatial barns, splendid carriages, pianos and pictures, silks and laces, summer tours, — all the accompaniments of opulence, they must have; and when the money was not on hand it was borrowed. Going at this gait, what wonder that, by the sudden halt of an unprosperous year or two, many of them have been thrown into bankruptcy?

What has happened to these neighbors of ours is what is happening on a larger scale to the whole people. Encouraged by the unsubstantial prosperity created by the increase of paper money, many of us have been living at too rapid a rate; and we find ourselves either badly in debt, or else in sore straits because we cannot keep our incomes up to the scale of expenditure we have established.

For the same reason, many extravagant business ventures have been taken. There seemed for a while to be no end to the money with which to build mills and factories and railroads: so we have rushed ahead, multiplying our manufacturing facilities beyond all reasonable demand for them, building railroads that go nowhere in particular, and sinking our easily gotten gains in bottomless enterprises.

Well, here we are, at the end of our tether. Business is dull, salaries are cut down, workmen are out of work; and that revival of trade, prophesied and waited for so eagerly for now these five years, does not come. What are we going to do about it?

Many remedies have been suggested. "Inflate the currency," say some. "Give us more money: money is all we need." That is all very well; but please remember that notes of hand, promises to pay, are not money. We shall not get out of our straits by giving or taking irredeemable paper. Our present troubles have arisen in great measure from the delusion that money-values can be manufactured with printing-presses. More of the same delusion will not cure us. When the toper gets up in the morning, dizzy and dejected, he thinks that what he wants is another glass of grog, and he generally goes and gets it; but it does not cure him.

Others advise the stoppage of production. It is not poverty, but the embarrassment of riches, that troubles us, they say. And if we could all make up our minds to wait a little while, till we have used up the stock on hand, things would go on again briskly. But if waiting a little while would do us a little good, I cannot see why waiting a long while would not do us more good; and on this principle, if all the people in the world should sit down and suck their thumbs for ten years, they would all, at the end of that time, be on the high road to fortune. Perhaps, however, it is not a general but a partial stoppage of business

that is recommended. But who shall stop? Moreover, those who cease from their labor must live, of
course, while they are waiting. Who will support
them?

No: the notion that the idleness of all or of any
would give us easier times, is one of the flimsiest of
delusions. It may be that some branches of production are overworked. If so, part of those who find
employment in them had better turn their hands to
something else; but we shall not mend matters by
sitting down and waiting. Why, suppose that in
every branch of industry the over-production was so
great that the supply of every thing was enormously
in excess of the demand for it, — so much in excess
that all the ordinary and extraordinary objects of
desire could be obtained as air and water and light
are obtained, without money and without price; so
that houses and furniture, and pictures and books, and
food and clothing, and horses and carriages were to
be had for the asking. Would the times be hard
then? Morally they would, no doubt; for the whole
people, liberated for a time from the need of work,
would betake themselves to all sorts of mischief: but
economically nobody would be likely to esteem such
times as those hard times. The nearer we can
approximate to that condition of things, the easier
will be our finances. And we approximate to this

6

condition, not by sitting still and waiting, but by working diligently to increase the world's store of wealth; by working, of course, so far as we are able, to supply those things of which there is the greatest deficiency, and for which there is the greatest demand.

The remedies we have mentioned are pure quackery. By no such superficial method shall we ever cure our complaint. The process of recovery will be slow, and it cannot be greatly hastened. The analysis we have made of the causes of the hard times shows this very clearly. You don't recover from a typhoid fever in twenty-four hours; not even with the aid of quack-doctors and travelling medicine-men. What, then, are the only effectual remedies?

In the first place, in direct contradiction to that counsel we were considering a moment ago, let everybody keep at work if he is now employed; or, if not, find something to do, and go at it. If too many are working at your particular trade or calling, so that you cannot get a living by it, find if you can some other occupation, even though it may be less congenial, that will give you a livelihood, and go to work in that. Don't sit round, whoever you are, waiting for something to turn up. Take hold of something, and turn it up. Shovel dirt, saw wood, do any kind of reputable work, rather than abide in idleness. Your work, if it be honest work, will not only replenish your own revenues, but it will help to make the whole community richer, and thus to hasten the return of better times.

Perhaps you feel yourself incapable of any other kind of work than that you have followed hitherto. It is one of the drawbacks of our present system of dividing and subdividing labor, that the industrial training of our workmen is kept within very narrow limits, and men are incapacitated for any variety of pursuits. One who has spent all his days in filing the point of a screw, or in making the head of a pin, hardly knows what to do when there are no more screws to file, or pins to head. Fertility of resource is a trait of American character that is decaying, I fear. The number of those who are Yankees by trade, and work at it, is not so large as once it was. We must try to keep out of this bondage to a single branch of work. We must not forget how to "turn ourselves," — a good old Yankee phrase. We must keep our eyes and ears open, and our hands practised too, if we can, in more than one kind of work. "Some things can be done, as well as others."

You will not all relish the suggestion, but the truth is that a good many of you must go back to the work of farming. The mills and the shops and the stores are not now, and will not soon be, able to furnish with employment all of those who have hitherto been supported by them ; and there are hundreds of thousands of work-people and trades-people in our towns who must find employment on the farms. The prospect may not be a pleasant one, but the alternative is starvation.

One hundred years ago the cities of the United States contained only one-thirtieth of the population: now one-fifth of all our people are in the cities. The growth of our city population has been quite too rapid for the national health.

Toward the large commercial and manufacturing towns, the tide of population has been steadily pouring now these many years. Farm-life is dull and solitary, farm-work is irksome and fatiguing, the gains of farming are slow: therefore the young men and the young women have deserted the farms, and have sought employment in the shops and the stores and the factories. All over New England, the rural districts have been depopulated ; in hundreds of outlying towns there are fewer inhabitants to-day than there were twenty years ago. The old houses where the fathers of the present generation lived and throve are falling down in ruins ; thousands of acres that once were under tillage are covered now with brushwood. Of those who began life on these New

England farms, a part have emigrated to the West, but a large number are in the Eastern cities and villages. City life has for the mercurial Yankee a strong attraction. He likes to mix with the crowd; he wants to be within reach of the telegraph-office and the daily journal; he greatly prefers his sensations fresh and at first hand. What is more, possibilities of rapid accumulation are not found upon the farms: it is only in the combinations of commercial life that they are revealed; and though the statistics show that the prizes in this lottery are few compared with the blanks, every true-born American cherishes a lively faith that a prize will come to him. At any rate, he wants to be on hand when the wheel goes round.

For all these reasons the agricultural districts of the East have been steadily losing their population, and the towns have been growing at their expense. Even during the period of inflation, many of these ambitious fortune-seekers have gained but a precarious livelihood; and now multitudes of them are out of work and out of funds, and their credit is growing poorer every day. The fact they must look in the face is just this: that trade is going to recover very slowly; that a great many factories and stores are closing, and will not open again for many a day; and that the clerks and operatives, male and

5

female, who have been supported by them, must get their living in some other way, or starve.

By the great majority of these the thought of seeking employment in the country is never entertained. I lately heard a young man, who had long been looking in vain for a clerkship, say that if he did not soon succeed he should try to get a situation as conductor on a horse-car. He did not seem to be aware that thousands of other young men in the same condition are piteously begging for the same kind of work, and that there would scarcely be room in the horse-cars for all the idle clerks and operatives to ride.

The thought of turning away from the excitements of town-life to the coarse fare, the hard work, and the plodding life of the farm, may be unwelcome; but would not this be infinitely better than the anxious and aimless life which many of you are leading? If you are compelled to work for wages, the money that you will receive for a month's labor on the farm will not be much; but you will have your board, your clothing will cost you but little, your other personal expenses will be next to nothing, and you can save nearly all of the money that you receive. The work of the farm is much less severe than it used to be when some of us were boys; and the conditions of the farmer's life are in many ways less narrow and hard than once they were; but even if this were not

the case, the young man who would not work on a
farm for ten dollars a month and his keeping, rather
than hang about the city waiting for work, begging
or borrowing the means of subsistence, or running
up a board-bill that he has no visible means of paying, is a poor specimen of manhood.

If you have a little money left, or can get a little
credit, there are plenty of farms that can be bought
at extremely low figures. With hard work and
prudent management you can obtain a living upon
such a place, and lay by something every year. The
prices of produce, especially of dairy produce, and
of fruits and vegetables as well, are high enough in
all our markets to afford any farmer who raises them
a good living.

But you say that the farmers talk about hard times
quite as loudly as the people in the towns, and that
many of them are heard complaining that they cannot
get a living. That may be true; but the farmers,
like all the rest of us, have been living extravagantly; they have mortgaged their farms for large
sums to obtain luxuries they could not afford; and
now they find it hard to pay the interest on these
mortgages, and keep up the scale of expenditure to
which they have accustomed themselves. If they
would be content to live as plainly as the farmers

used to live thirty years ago, they could meet their expenses and pay their debts.

The opportunity that is offered to the idle people of the cities, of becoming proprietors and cultivators of the soil, is one they cannot afford to overlook. They ought to understand that the gains of agriculture are slow; that it is only by hard labor and great prudence that any savings are made; but industry and economy, united with good judgment, will insure any household a comfortable and sure support. And no remedy for the hard times would be more radical than a transfer of the unemployed multitudes of our town population to productive labor upon the farms.

In the second place, whether you live in the city or in the country, you must reverse the bad tendencies of the past years, and practise economy. Learn the wickedness of waste, and avoid it; learn the duty of living within your means, and do it. The scale of expenditure needs revising in many quarters among poor folks, and among poor rich folks too. There are carriages, fineries, all sorts of luxurious accompaniments of life, that must be heroically discontinued.

Perhaps some of you working-people may be inclined to say that you never indulge in any superfluities. I don't know about that. The bare necessaries of life cost very little. Henry Thoreau, the

Concord hermit, has shown us just how expensive they are. His living for eight months, in the house built with his own hands in Walden woods, cost him $33.87¼, — a little more than four dollars a month! He gives us all the figures; and we can take his word for their accuracy, for he was an honest man. Those were not starved and barren months by any means: when he was not working in his bean-field, he was busy with his books, or studying with quick and sympathetic appreciation the wonderful things in the world around him; and the result is a book that will rank very high among the products of American literature.

Still I would not counsel you to try living in a fashion quite so primitive as his. You do not want to deny yourselves all the comforts of life; and you have a perfect right to take pleasure in some things that most men regard as luxuries. You ought not to starve your minds, for one thing. If you are ever to be emancipated utterly from bondage to toil, it will be through mental training. Your tastes that are intellectual or spiritual you ought to develop; and I counsel you to do so, even if you are obliged to wear plainer clothes, to deny yourselves several circuses and nigger-minstrel shows in the course of the year, and to put yourselves on very short allowance of tobacco and rum.

In the third place, it is good counsel to forbear comparing your lot with that of your more fortunate neighbors. Many of our discomforts are relative, not positive. It is not always because you are in absolute want that you are troubled: it is often because others about you have many things that you have not. If you could be put, with your present straitened income, into a neighborhood where all the people were poorer than yourself, you would be much less distressed on account of its straitness. Times would be easier with you right away.

In the fourth place, it may be that, without much thinking of your neighbors, you are very much in the habit of looking upon objects that are beyond your reach, and worrying because you cannot have them. It is the things you have not and cannot get that you think about most. How would it do to think a little more of what you have, or may have, and a little less of what you cannot have? Wouldn't it make times easier with you if you gave more study to what you can get out of your income, and less to what you can't get out of it? I want to take this counsel to myself while I commend it to you. Suppose we all say to ourselves, "This year, or this month, we shall have to spend on our living so much; that is all we can count on. Now, let us see how far we can make it go; how much good we can get out of it, — how many comforts for the home, how much culture, how much stimulus for what is best in our natures, how much bounty wherewith to make other hearts glad who are in worse straits than we are." There is an immense amount of happiness, and profit too, to be derived from very small revenues, if one sets to work in that way to utilize them. This philosophy is as old as the days of Diogenes, but it needs to be enforced upon every generation.

Doubtless you think that my prescription for your financial ills is a very simple one, and indeed it is; but if you will try it faithfully, I know it will do you good; and I haven't much faith in any other mode of treatment. The whole country has been waiting for a sensational revival of business, but it will not come. The only relief for our present distresses will come through industry and frugality; through a chastening of our ambitious notions of life, and the cultivation of simpler tastes and a more contented spirit.

And, if to contentment we can add godliness, that, I have authority for saying, will be a great gain. What I mean by this is the bearing of our burdens, whether they be of wealth or of want, as in the sight of God. The maxims of a sound philosophy are not to be despised: they serve us often for guidance in this world. But there is something better than philosophy; and that is the knowledge that, over all these affairs of ours, One is watching whose wisdom is perfect to direct, whose strength is infinite to keep and to deliver. If we can only come into that assurance; if we can only believe with all our hearts, that our heavenly Father loves us and cares for us; that, so long as we place our confidence in him and try to do his will, nothing can go amiss with us, — we shall not have any more hard times. " Trust in the Lord, and do good: so shalt thou dwell in the land, and verily thou shalt be fed." If you will only believe that, and make that faith the central principle of your life, all these hard questions about the wherewithal of life will cease to vex your soul. You may not be rich; but you will know, as Paul knew, how to be in want as well as how to abound; and one kind of knowledge is worth just as much as the other, has just the same sweet comfort in it.

I do not mean that this trust will ever release you from diligence or prudence: I mean that when you have done your best, and chosen the path that seems to you safest, it will deliver you from anxiety and despondency, and fill your soul with a perfect peace. If you can find this sure support, and rest upon it, the sting will be taken from your troubles. When the work stops, and the supplies are cut off, and the little hoard is shrinking, it is good to think that there is One who knows all about our needs, and who has promised to take care of us if we will commit our lives to him. To say that there is rest and comfort by and by for those who trust in him, is to tell but part ·of the truth: there is rest and comfort for them here and now.

## IV.

## RISING IN THE WORLD.

For the virtue of thrift, the duty of rising in the world, we may find good warrant in high places. There is not only a command to work in the Decalogue, but there are many other commands scattered through the Bible, which set before us our duty to live and thrive by our work. The first word spoken to man by his Maker was a command to replenish the earth, and subdue it, — to fill it not only with inhabitants, but with wealth for the use of its inhabitants. Along with all the warnings against setting our hearts on riches, and putting our trust in them, there are many other commands, which either expressly or by implication recognize it as a duty that every man owes to himself, to his household, and to his neighbors, to strive after temporal prosperity.

74

Not to mention the exhortations found in the New
Testament epistles and in the Psalms of David, we
have one whole book, the Book of Proverbs, whose
inspiration is not generally questioned, in which the
duty to be diligent and prosper is set forth with a
boundless wealth of illustration.

It is a duty that many of you do not need to be
instructed in. The fault of the great majority of
those who hear me is not that they do not value
prosperity enough, but that they value it far too
highly; not that they have no ambition to rise in the
world, but that this ambition absorbs their energies
and consumes their lives. The lazy races of the
Orient are in far greater need of Solomon's pungent
proverbs about slothfulness and thriftlessness than the
eager, pushing people of New England can possibly
be. The motives to accumulation are always present
in our society, and need to be supplied by suggestions to very few minds.

There are several errors, however, concerning this
matter, into which men are led by their eagerness
and their indolence, and which it may be well to
notice. The working people before me — most if
not all of them — are anxious enough to prosper;
but it is not at all improbable that the ideas of many
of them, as to what prosperity is, are somewhat incor-
rect; and that some, if called on to tell what rising

in the world implies, would give loose and crude definitions.

In the minds of some persons, this notion may be lurking, that rising in the world involves the cessation of labor. They are hoping, in time, to rise so high that they shall be above work. In the happy elevation to which they hope to climb, the noises of tools and the clatter of machinery are no more heard. Now, this, as we saw in the first chapter, is a false view of life. It is not by going up the ladder of true progress and prosperity, but by going down, that one gets away from work. In the scale of advancement that God has marked for the race, there is no place where work is omitted. Money may deliver one over to idleness, and sometimes does; but let him remember, when he gets there, that, since he left the point where he stood when he worked every day for his living, he has been going the downward road.

You do not rise in the world by ceasing to be a producer, or a helper of your fellows. Your powers of body and of mind were given you to be used with steady and beneficent purpose; and you do not rise by suffering them to rust in indolence, or to run to waste in constant pleasuring. Whoever lives without work is living a dependent life, — a pauper life, indeed, whether he lives in a poorhouse or in a palace.

There is essental degradation in such a life as that; and they are to be pitied who have gone down to it, whether they went down by the road of penury or the road of plenty.

All the material comforts and values that are enjoyed by persons who consider themselves able to live without labor must be procured for them by labor; cannot be produced in any other way. The food, the apparel, the dwelling, the furniture, all that supports and adorns life, is the product of labor. The labor of the farmer, the miner, the fisherman, the lumberman, produces the raw materials of wealth; the labor of the artisan turns them into useful forms; the labor of the merchant and the common carrier transports and distributes and exchanges them; the labor of the banker provides for the transfer and re-distribution of the money that constitutes the medium of exchange; and so on, in a thousand ways not mentioned, men are working together to increase the store of the world's possessions.

So also, as regards the immaterial wealth of the world, the stock of knowledge and truth that the world contains: it is all the product of labor. True, there is knowledge that comes by inspiration; but not even this, as men now are, can be turned to account for the purposes of life, without hard work. The greater part of the knowledge the world contains is acquired and disseminated by labor. To some is given the work of original investigation in science or in philosophy; to others, the work of research into the lore of past ages; to others, the work of criticism; to others, the work of teaching: to all, the duty of standing up for the truth so far as it is known, of waging warfare upon ignorance and iniquity, of publishing salvation from the lust of the flesh and the lust of the eye and the pride of life. And this is work certainly not less honorable or productive than that of the farmer or the artisan. Its products are not seen and temporal: they are unseen and eternal; but they are not therefore valueless.

In one or the other of these two great classes of workers, — those who are adding to the material wealth of the world, or those who are enhancing its immaterial treasures, — every able-bodied and sound-minded adult human being ought to be found. We are all bound together in society by a bond so close, a relation so intimate, that each is affected by the unfaithfulness of every other. If any man commits a crime, he injures not only himself and the person against whom the crime was committed and the immediate circle of kinsfolk or acquaintance, but he injures every other person in the land; for he does what he can to make society less secure and life less desirable. So, if a person lives in indolence, it matters not how large his accumulations may be, the whole community is the loser by his course. He is adding nothing to the stock of the world's posses- sions: he is doing what he can, and that is some- times a vast deal, to diminish their quantity; he is a destroyer, instead of being a producer. From the great commonwealth of workers, which ought to in- clude all men, he is an alien. In the best state of society no such person will be found.

Just here one mistake must be pointed out. There are many, who to a superficial view might seem to be idle, that are really industrious and useful workers. The proprietor of a large manufacturing establishment may be regarded by the girl that works at the loom as a very lazy man. He sits in his office, and talks; he rides round in his carriage; he goes down to the city now and then; he seems, to some of the hands in the mill, to have a very easy time: whereas the fact may be that no person in his employ works so hard as he does. ⌈One of the most useful as well as one of the most difficult and weari- some kinds of work is to organize work for others.⌋ Those who are actively and successfully carrying on business are not idle, though they may perform but little manual labor. The woman who organizes and manages prudently the work of a large household may be a diligent and useful worker, even though she may not do any large share of the housework with her own hands.

It is not therefore of such as these that I am speaking ; but rather of those who by inheritance or by previous acquisition have gained property which gives them an income, and who are doing nothing but amusing themselves. This is a kind of life that some are leading, and for which many are longing. It is not the right kind of life to live, and it is a foolish thing to long for it.

Others think to rise in the world by exchanging the calling in which they have been trained for some other which to them seems more honorable. An ambitious young mechanic says to himself, " As a mere skilled laborer I never can amount to any thing : if I am to rise in the world, I must get into something else, — into mercantile life, or into one of the learned professions." But such a change as this is by no means certain to be a change for the better. The mechanic may be well fitted to excel in his calling, and totally unfit for the calling to which he aspires ; and, if this be the case, he is not elevated, but rather degraded by the change. A good tin- smith is not rising in the world when he becomes a poor lawyer. A good bricklayer is going down, not up, when he makes of himself an indifferent journalist. When a first-rate shoemaker turns into a fourth-rate preacher, he throws himself away. No calling can be so sacred or so honorable as to confer distinction upon a man not qualified to discharge its duties. All good work is honorable and sacred ; all poor, slipshod work is despicable and profane : and in the callings that are most responsible and influential, it is even more to be detested than in those that are less conspicuous.

It is therefore not clear that if you abandon one calling, and choose another which to you seems higher, you will be going upward. Your elevation is determined not so much by the *kind* of work you are doing (provided always it is honest work) as by the *way* you are doing it. The highest calling in which you can engage is the one whose work you can do best.

It ought not to be necessary to add that no man can truly be said to rise who by dishonorable means gains for himself wealth, or notoriety, or power. To none but fools does such a career ever seem to be any thing but a swift decline and a fatal fall. The theatric height to which the bad man thus attains is not only ·to all right vision the means for displaying his own disgrace, but it is certain in the end to appear so even to the fools that once applauded him.

Not many years ago, there lived in the city of New York a chairmaker — a fairly decent man, no doubt —

6

by the name of Tweed. Dissatisfied with his calling, and ambitious to rise in the world, he took to politics. By all the black arts known to the politician of the period, he rose rapidly to power. The metropolis of the continent was subject to his will: he dictated its laws, he appointed its magistrates and judges, he filled his lap with wealth plundered from its treasury. Not only within the metropolis, but throughout the State and the nation, his power was felt and feared; he was thought able — this cabinet-maker — not only to make municipal and gubernatorial and even presidential chairs, but to fill them with the creatures of his choice. They began to talk of erecting a brazen image of him down in New York; and there were plenty that were making ready to fall down and worship it. "Behold the eminence," many fools were crying, "to which this man has climbed!" And everywhere base men began to do likewise. The same bad arts everywhere began to creep into our politics. To use the rumshops and the ruffians in corrupting the voters and packing the caucuses; to manipulate all the vile elements of society in such a manner that the ballot-box should paralyze the intelligent will of the people, instead of expressing it, — this began to be only too common; and good men either spoke lightly of it, as one of the inseparable accompaniments of politics, or else shook their heads gravely, and said, "It's all wrong, but what can you do? You can't help yourselves. Look at Tweed and his Ring!"

But how long did they stand on that bad eminence to be looked at, the wonder-stock of fools, the scorn of wise men? Only a very little space. The cup of their iniquities, how soon it was full! And then the breath of God's avenging wrath blew upon them; and now where are they? The once proud imperator, stripped of his honors, driven from his offices, hides, a condemned convict, from the sight of men; he who once had his choice of palaces now counts it a great mercy that he may choose among prisons; his property is scattered; his house is desolate; his fellow-conspirators are fugitives and vagabonds in the earth.

Ay, look at Tweed and his Ring! Look, all you base politicians, who have striven to copy in your small way his bad example! Look, all you cowardly citizens, who think such things are inseparable from politics and cannot be helped! Look, all you lowly mechanics and laborers, who are discontented sometimes with your condition, and burn to rise, no matter how, to higher places! Look, and learn that the stars in their courses fight against the man that makes war upon righteousness; and that there is no pit so deep as that into which the creature falls, who, like Lucifer, would climb to place and power by defying the immutable laws of God.

If, then, one may not wish to rise above labor, nor to exchange a calling in which he excels for one in which he must fail, nor to attain wealth or station by dishonorable means, what is meant by rising in the world? What is included in the just ambition of thrifty working-people?

1. To be out of debt, for one thing. It is sometimes necessary to incur debts; when this has been done, the first business is to pay them. You do not rise in the world by getting finery and furniture wherewith to make a brave show, while unpaid bills are hanging like millstones around your neck. Nothing holds a man down like debt. You will not rise very high till you are rid of it.

2. If you are in discomfort, or absolute wretchedness, your endeavor ought to be to rise out of it into a condition of comfort. It is hard to draw the line here, for one would be satisfied with a manner of life in which another would be wretched. Still we all know that some measure of decency and seemliness is possible to all in this land. It is not necessary for human beings to live like dogs in a kennel, neither is it necessary for them to live like princes in a palace; between these two extremes there is a golden mean of respectability within which we may all abide.

Though elegance may be beyond our reach, cleanliness is not; and that is a grace that must not be lightly esteemed. If our attire is neat, and our apartments are orderly and tidy, this will go a long way toward making up for any lack of stylishness or costliness in our raiment and our furniture. I have found the kitchens of some working-people very pleasant places to sit and talk in. All of us may hope to rise in the world high enough to get out of the dirt.

Beyond this, it appears to me that working-people ought always to try to lay by something; not with the thought that they may be rich enough in the future to live in idleness, but that they may have a provision made against sickness or infirmity or old age. For one thing, they should keep it before them, as a chief purpose of life, that they will at some time have homes of their own. A little spot of this earth's surface in which he may feel the honest pride of ownership, a roof that may shelter him in his declining days, — these are not, I trust, beyond the attainment, as they ought not to be beyond the expectation, of the thrifty laboring-man. Having procured for himself a home, it will be well if in some safe place he shall lay up for himself a good foundation against the time to come; so that if disaster overtake him, and his supplies are cut off, he may not be left in absolute penury.

But some of you will tell me that even this moderate measure of prosperity is not easy of attainment. It is as much as you can do, you say, to live decently on your earnings: the prospect of accumulating any thing is very slight indeed. And you think that if you are ever to achieve any degree of independence, you must rise from the ranks of the wage-laborers into the ranks of the employers of labor. But it is by no means certain that you would improve your condition by such an attempt. Some journeymen doubtless have the qualities that would fit them to succeed as employers. They have organizing ability: they could plan work judiciously, could make close estimates and wise investments, could judge of men and materials and times and tendencies and work and results, and therefore could do well as masters and contractors. But there are others, and these are greatly in the majority, who, though skilful workmen, are lacking in this power to organize work. While they are employed as workmen, they do admirably: when they attempt to take the direction of work, they are sure to fail. It is not the easiest thing in the world, even if one has some capital to begin with, to carry on successfully an industrial or a mercantile business.

I shall be asked if this admission does not take the ground from under the system of co-operation. If it be true that only a few workmen have the ability to manage business, would not a business that was managed by a body of workmen be badly managed? The same query applies to a town government. Only a few of all the voters of a town have the executive ability necessary to manage the town affairs. Yet the business of the towns of this Commonwealth has, as a rule, been very well conducted. The voters generally have sense enough to select capable men, and intrust the business to them. I don't know why co-operation in the business of making shoes, for example, should be deemed quixotic, when co-operation in the business of government — a business infinitely more complex and delicate — has been demonstrated by an experience of two hundred and fifty years in Massachusetts to be wholly practicable.

Of course successful co-operation, whether in the state or the shop, requires intelligence in the co-operators; sense enough to know when they are well served, to choose wise representatives, to give them some discretion, and to trust them in the exer cise of it. The fact that the experiment has broken down so often proves just this and nothing more: that the working-men who have tried it have lacked this modicum of sense.  And while I have no doubt that there will be many more such failures, before there will be any general prevalence of the system, yet it seems only natural to hope for a degree of intelligence and self-control among our workmen that shall render them capable of combining their savings as capital, and becoming proprietors as well as laborers.

In the mean time let those who have the will to better their condition try what virtue there is in industry, and thoroughness, and fidelity, and economy. Work patiently; perfect yourselves as workmen; learn to do your work in the very best manner. Stand at the top of your calling.  There is always room higher up.  You can become so skilful, so competent, so trustworthy, that your services shall always be in demand at the highest rate of wages. If you will then husband your resources, deny yourselves fooleries and fineries that you would be better off without, and take good care of your savings, you may greatly improve your condition, even though the prospect of a competence may not be very clear.

It may be well to face the fact that, for the great majority of you, there is nothing better than this in store.  Some of you, doubtless, are hoping for something that seems to you a great deal better.  You are in perpetual discomfort and discontent, burdened

perhaps with debts that do not diminish, or living at
best from hand to mouth, no better off at the end of
the year than you were at the beginning; and you
are hoping to rise out of this condition into an easier
and better one, but how or when you do not exactly
know. Some of you have great expectations, that
some good fortune will come to you; that somebody
will die, and remember you in his will; that you will
discover a gold-mine or an oil-well somewhere; that
you will run across some streak of good luck; that
in some exceptional and fortuitous way you will
rise in the world. The sooner you rid yourselves of
this delusion, the better. The chances are a hundred
thousand to one that nothing of the sort will ever
happen to you. If you and I are ever to be better
off than we are, if prosperity is ever to come to us,
it will not come by luck, but by industry and economy. Standing right where we are, taking the means
within our reach, we are to achieve all the prosperity
that will ever be ours.

To some of you, it may seem that the prospect I
have held up before you is not a very brilliant one.
To be able by hard work and close economy to get
out of debt and want, to make yourself possessor of
a comfortable home, and to have a little hoard laid
by in the savings bank, and yet to toil on from year
to year at the same vocation: if this is rising in the

world, you say, it is not rising very high, assuredly. Possibly your own ambition has taken much loftier flights. Possibly you thought that I would hold up before you the examples of the men of our time, or of former times, who have risen out of poverty into great wealth or high station, and would pique your ambition by the story of their rapid advancement, reminding you that the paths they trod to these eminences invite your feet. But I must own to you that the heights to which I long to see you rise are not these at all. God knows I wish you well, every one of you; and if by wishing it I could secure your highest welfare, none of you would wait for it long. But looking at the world from my point of view, I am not sure that, if I had the lamp of Aladdin, I would put you in the place of Stewart or of Vanderbilt. There are advantages for the attainment of the highest end of life to men who stand where they do; but the drawbacks more than balance the advantages. It is an awful trial to which any man's soul is exposed, when he is given vast wealth, — wealth that enables him to gild or to conceal vice; wealth that absorbs his affections, and dulls, if it does not destroy, his sense of responsibility. And while all our millionaires show that they have power of a certain kind, — shrewdness, organizing ability, force of will, — I fear we must say of the most of them that

outside of the world of finance and exchanges they
are very small indeed. They know one thing
thoroughly, — that is, how to accumulate property;
and they know very little else. When thought turns
toward them, on what does it fasten? Is it not the
merchandise or the gold that they have heaped up?
Is there any thing in the personality of such men
that fascinates us? Do they not rather chill and
repel our affection? When we measure them by
ethical or by spiritual standards, the only ones we
shall think of applying to ourselves when we come
to sum up life and see what it has amounted to, we
find their stature is not great.

I look over the towns where my homes have been,
and see here and there a plain working-man who goes
to his work in the winter mornings before the sun is
up, and sups with his family by candlelight after his
day's work is done; who has a snug little home of
his own, and a small hoard in a safe place; who
has a wife to whom in heart and life he has always
been loyal, and a little brood of children that he
loves and watches tenderly; a man who, though not
college-bred, has large information gained through
reading, and ready wit and quick perceptions and
wide sympathies, and who lives a pure and happy
life every day before God and man; and I say to
myself, " I wonder, now, if that fellow would change

places *and souls* with such a man as — well, never
mind his name; would take the old millionaire's
millions, and along with them his shrivelled conscience, and his sordid desires, and his narrow views
of life and destiny, and his haunting memories of
treachery and foul play. I wonder if this honest
sound-hearted working-man would, if he could, make
such an exchange as this. If he could and should,
he would prove himself to be a miserable fool. O,
who is so blind as not to see that the portion of such
a working-man is infinitely more to be coveted than
that of such a millionaire?

Prosperity, my friends, prosperity in a very moderate measure, but not affluence, I covet for myself
and for you. There is a better life than that to which
abundance is wont to lead; and to that every one
of you may attain. To stand in your lot with stead-
fastness; to take the good of life with thankfulness,
and its evil with patience; to do your daily work
cheerfully and well; to cherish those whom God has
given you with a pure affection; to receive with
open and vigilant mind all the truth that is brought
you; to love and help your neighbors as you have
opportunity; and to hold communion every day with
Him whose grace will make you strong to endure
and overcome, — is there any higher life than this
possible to any of us?

Good friends, I wish I could make you all believe that a man's life does not consist in the abundance of the things he possesses. I wish I could make you all see that it is possible for you, standing right where you are, to realize the very highest ideal of true living. I wish you all knew that by your fidelity, your contentment, your manliness, your steadfast choice of spiritual rather than temporal good, you might clothe this work-day life of yours with a glory such as seldom shines in courts and palaces. The multitudes about you are racing after pelf and place, — scheming and striving and rioting. God help you to see that there are higher ends than these they aim at! God save you from the leanness of soul that is their sure portion, and show you that you need not wish for any better sphere in which to achieve true greatness than that in which he has placed you!

# V.

## THE HOUSEHOLD AND THE HOME.

The family is the oldest of the institutions of society, and the most sacred; it is before and above the Church and the State. If there is any thing absolutely fundamental and essential in social order, it is the family.

Yet any one who carefully watches the drift of public movements must be aware of a wide-spread conspiracy against this venerable and divine institution. The workings of this conspiracy appear partly in certain startling social experiments now being tried in various parts of our land, and partly in certain tendencies that show themselves everywhere in society, moving sometimes upon and sometimes beneath the surface.

The extreme measure of religious liberty enjoyed

94

in America has resulted in a variety of social monstrosities. Shakerism, Oneida Communism, Mormonism, are ostensibly and fundamentally religions, and are tolerated here only as religions. There is need that this whole subject of the toleration of religious systems should be re-examined. When such a social abomination as the Oneida or the Wallingford Community springs up in the midst of civilized society, and claims to be protected on the ground that it is a form of religion, it is high time that we were considering just how much immorality and corruption can be covered by a creed. Otherwise we may by and by witness the rising-up of sects divinely commissioned to commit arson and murder and highway robbery.

It is the peculiarity of the societies referred to, that they repudiate the family relation, and substitute for it a phalanx or a community or a harem. This is the error on which they are built, the crime against society that they are organized to perpetrate. No substitute for the family has been or can be provided without turning earth into hell; and whoever attempts to put such theories into organic form ought to be restrained by law as an evil-doer.

Concerning the Shakers, this judgment ought perhaps to be tempered somewhat. All that needs to be said about them is, that their social theories are unnatural and absurd; that if they live up to them they will get but few followers, and do but little harm; and that, until it becomes plain that they are making their theories the cover of debaucheries, the State had better let them alone.

But it is not only among the Communists and the Mormons that the enemies of the family are found. The agitation now in progress in behalf of suffrage for woman is carried on in part by persons who have no respect for the family. Of those who are active in this movement, very many are wholly innocent of any design upon the stability of the household; they think, and so do I, that the enfranchisement of women may be consistent with the maintenance of the family. But there are some that make no secret of their contempt for the present order of things; they speak of marriage and maternity as if they thought them bondage and degradation, and openly counsel young women never to marry.

The conspiracy against the family counts still other conspirators, of a very different class. The whole tendency of social life in some circles is such as to discourage wedlock. The extravagant and luxurious habits of life that have become so prevalent lead many to shrink from assuming the expense of a family. Knowing that it would not be possible for them, with the incomes at their disposal, to maintain a certain elaborate style of life, which to them seems the very minimum of respectability, many young persons deliberately resolve on single life. The young man makes up his mind that a wife is a luxury too expensive for him to afford; and the young woman resolves that she will not marry unless there is money enough in the proffered hand to support her in good style. Thus the young woman grows mercenary and frivolous, and the young man dissolute and rakish. Every year that passes makes it less probable that they will ever enter into the family relations, and still less probable that, if they do, this relation will be a happy one.

This state of things, which we witness everywhere in the middle classes, is greatly to be deplored. It is the source of a large part of the vice and wretchedness with which these classes are infested. Multitudes of people have high notions and limited means; and they are always indefinitely postponing the beginning of the family life, simply because they are such arrant cowards that they dare not live in smaller and less richly furnished apartments, dare not wear plainer clothes, than some of their neighbors. I do not think that working-people are so apt as people of other classes to be governed by these mercenary considerations. They are generally content to begin life as they can afford to begin; humbly, and in the

7

faith that they can improve their circumstances as time goes on. I hope this will always remain true of them. There are doubtless exceptions, as in the case of persons of infirm health, in which such responsibilities should not be assumed; but marriage, and early marriage, ought to be the expectation and the purpose. There ought to be manhood and womanhood enough in the married pair to enable them to begin their family life in a very humble way, to live within their means, if their means are very limited. The practice of putting off the day till the life can begin in elegance and splendor, is a most heartless and abominable practice.

" It is not good for man that he should be alone," was the word of the Creator in Eden. It may be the duty of some and the misfortune of others to live singly ; but that is not the divine rule for mankind. *"It is not good for man* that he should be alone." Outside of the family, he is exposed to a thousand temptations from which the family would shield him.

I know that the safeguards of the home, the motives furnished by the household, are not sufficient to restrain some men from iniquity. But, with the great majority of decent people, domestic life is a powerful check upon the baser passions. There are husbands and fathers among my readers living sober and reputable lives to-day, who would, if it were not for their families, be walking in the path of indulgence. The thought of the wife and the children at home, the unwillingness to bring shame or dishonor upon their families, is always present in their minds to lead them in the ways of virtue. And since this motive does operate so powerfully upon every man of honor, it is wise for every man who desires to preserve his purity of heart and of life to put himself under its influence.

But not only is it not good for man that he should be alone: it is good for him that he should dwell in the family relation. The family serves not only as a restraint: it serves also as a stimulus; it furnishes a powerful reinforcement to all that is good in human nature. Certain of the virtues, and they are the most beautiful of all the virtues, can hardly be acquired except in the family. The education that comes to both men and women in the school of the family is perhaps the most valuable education they ever receive. The husband and wife who are united by a true affection are brought into a relation that has no type or parallel in this world. The higher spiritual nature is enriched by wedlock with gifts that can be obtained in no other way. The perfect sympathy, the true accord, the entire identification of interests and hopes, that characterizes the happy married life, is the source of infinite blessing to both husband and wife. By their affection for each other they become assimilated in character and nature. Sometimes this likeness of spirit reveals itself even in the countenance, and as they grow older there comes to be in many cases a striking resemblance between them. But when this does not take place, there is often a wonderful interfusion of mental traits and characteristics. The husband learns, after a time, to see not only with his own eyes, but with those of his wife ; and the wife knows by a perfect intuition, what impression every circumstance or sentiment will make upon the mind of her husband. Now, this perfect blending of the two lives gives to each greater value, greater breadth, greater beauty. The manly character, in its noblest manifestation, is one-sided and incomplete; so is the womanly : a full and symmetrical development is not possible to either except as the two are brought together in a genuine and life-long union.

But the benefits of domestic life come not only from wedlock, but from parentage. No philosophy can measure, no language can tell, the good that children bring to their parents. When the pure fountains of parental love are opened in the heart, a new life is begun. New feelings, sober and tender and full of purifying grace, spring up in the soul ;

new visions are opened, new motives are supplied. He must be a cold-blooded miscreant indeed, who can receive from the great Father the gift of a little child, helpless, innocent, yet immortal, and not feel his heart stirred to its profoundest depths with joy and hope and solemn thankfulness. He must be hardened and imbruted beyond all hope of reformation, who can watch the growth of a little child, — the unfolding of its beauty, the dawnings of its intelligence, the venturings of its artless thought into the dark regions of human speculation, the pluming of the soul's pinions for heavenly flights, — with no new aspirations for a better life.

Such are some of the blessings that come to us through the family. The wholesome restraints it throws around us, the new and holy experiences to which it introduces us, the enlargement that it brings to the best part of our nature, all help to demonstrate that it is what Christians claim, — an institution of divine appointment. It may be to some the savor of death unto death; but so is the gospel of grace: rightly used, it can only be the savor of life unto life.

It may be, however, that these fundamental truths concerning family life are all accepted by you. If so, suffer a few words concerning the forming of the family, — the building of the home.

Some of you are looking forward to the time when you shall have families and homes of your own. It is by marriage that the household is constituted; and, as the initial organic rite, its sacredness can hardly be exaggerated. Your material prosperity and your moral and spiritual welfare depend upon your marriage more than upon any other event of your life. I hope, young people, that you always treat this great subject seriously; that you have resolved to govern all your conduct in relation to it, not by romantic notions, nor by mercenary purposes, nor by passionate impulses, but by the higher reason and the purer affections. Foolish choices have always been made, and doubtless always will be. It is not likely that I could give you any rules that would enable you to make an infallible selection; and it is still less likely that you would follow any rules that I could give you, if they were ever so good. It is a business that is rarely done by rule; nevertheless it is a business that should not be done recklessly. As a safe guide in the premises, let me suggest one simple maxim. Friendship as well as love, friendship even more than love, is the indispensable condition of true marriage. Friendship is the harmony of the higher elements of the nature, — of sentiments, tastes, pursuits; while by love is commonly meant only the attraction of passion. Remember, then, young man, that you want in a wife a friend; remember that she is to be your nearest and most intimate friend; and ask yourself whether it is likely that the one of whom you are thinking will answer all the conditions of a near and perpetual friendship. In short, supposing this person were of your own sex, would the expectation of a close and life-long intimacy between you be full of joy and promise? If you can soberly answer this question in the affirmative, you need ask no further questions; if you cannot, you had better pause.

When the important choice has been made, and consummated by marriage, then the family life begins. If the choice be a wise and happy one, the future is secure. But what if there was an error here? What if two are brought together in this relation who are imperfectly fitted, or wholly unfitted, by nature and by education, for each other? Such mistakes are made in all circles of society. What shall be done in such a case? There is one thing, and only one, that can be done, and that is to make the best of it. If the parties both discover after marriage that there is more discord than harmony in their union, that is certainly a great misfortune; but retreat is not possible. Tolerance, forbearance, are needed then. To dwell upon the hard fact, constantly to deplore it, is to fill life with wretchedness. The wise course is for each one heartily and hopefully to resolve that these discords shall be harmonized. When two pianos are brought together for the playing of a duet, one is almost always tuned a little higher than the other. If they were played together, the discord would be horrible; but the tuner, with a quick ear and a skilful hand, can soon bring them into harmony. When two lives are joined together in wedlock, it is very seldom that they are in perfect accord at the beginning; more or less tuning of both is commonly needed to make the harmony perfect. Sometimes it is a long and difficult task; but it is never impossible if only there be a steady purpose on both sides to accomplish it. This, then, is what must be done. Each must study the tastes and peculiarities of the other, must be patient with the infirmities of the other, must seek to increase the other's happiness in every possible way; and, above all, each must resolve to become better and more amiable every day; for the better these two persons are, the more certain they will be to agree.

Such an endeavor as this, quietly and cheerfully persisted in on both sides, will quickly substitute harmony for discord. There is abundant happiness in store for every unhappy couple that will heartily make this endeavor. Brooding over the mistakes of the past is poor business. The poet tells us that —

> " Of all sad words of tongue or pen,
> The saddest are these, ' It might have been!' "

They are often the silliest, too, as well as the saddest. If the time that is spent in lamenting past mistakes were turned to the improvement of present opportunities, many marred lives might be made beautiful.

There is a movement now in certain quarters (or *was*, for I think it has partly lost its head) to relax the stringency of the marriage bond, and to allow separation for slight causes, — for mere incompatibility of temper and taste. This would be a terrible mistake. The probable results of such a course, obvious enough to any sort of vision, should make us pause. Who could doubt that it would lead to greater recklessness in the forming of this relation? What might be so easily ended would oftener than now be lightly begun. Moreover, it would encourage and magnify disagreements. Many slight infelicities that now are patiently borne would, under such a state of things, be magnified into great grievances; and there would soon be little permanency in the family life. No, my friends; it is not by removing obstacles to separation, that we are to improve domestic life. Easy divorce is not the way to "home, sweet home:" it leads in exactly the opposite direction; it is the straight road to pandemonium.

The household having been formed, and fortified against the assaults of bad philosophy and fickle passion, the question of its rule next arises. What form of government shall prevail? Is the family a monarchy — or man-archy? Is the husband and father the lord and master, and are the wife and children his subjects and servants? You know how it *is* yourselves; what I want to know is, how it ought to be. The question is, of course, respecting the condition of the wife in the household. Ought she to be in a subject condition?

If we appeal to history, we shall find an easy answer. In the primitive barbarism, the woman is ranked with the lower animals, or but little above them. She is the property of the man. The father sells his daughters just as he does his domestic animals; and the husband buys his wife or wives as he buys his oxen or sheep. The Zulu fathers count each marriageable daughter as so many cattle. There is a regular price-current for wives, which rises and falls with the cattle-market. When cattle are scarce, wives are cheap; when cattle are plenty, wives are dear. That is what a Zulu husband means when he

speaks of his dear wife. Among these and other
barbarians, women have no social or civil rights at
all. A man may not kill a female belonging to the
family of his neighbor, because she is his neighbor's
property; but he may kill his own wife or daughter,
if he choose: has he not a right to do what he will
with his own?

Coming out of barbarism into the conditions of
civilization, we find the condition of the woman but
little altered for the better. "Until a later period in
European history," says Mr. Mill, "the father had
the right to dispose of his daughter in marriage at
his own will and pleasure, without any regard to
hers. The church, indeed, was so far faithful to a
better morality as to require a formal 'yes' from the
woman at the marriage ceremony; but there was
nothing to show that the consent was other than
compulsory. . . . After marriage, the man had an-
ciently (but this was anterior to Christianity) the
power of life and death over his wife. She could
invoke no law against him: he was her sole tribunal
and law. For a long time he could repudiate her,
but she had no corresponding power in regard to
him. By the old laws of England, the husband was
called the *lord* of the wife. He was literally
regarded as her sovereign, insomuch that the murder
of a man by his wife was called treason (*petty*, as

distinguished from *high* treason), and was more cruelly avenged than was usually the case with high treason; for the penalty was burning to death."

Such are some of the answers that history gives, when we inquire what has been the relation of woman to the family. With the advent of Christianity came a great mitigation in the hardships of her condition. The power of life and death was withdrawn from the husband, his right to discard and abandon his wife at pleasure was denied, and he was greatly restrained in the infliction upon her of physical injury. Yet it is not long since it was considered every husband's inalienable right to flog his wife, if she showed herself insubordinate. If, therefore, the thing that has been is the thing that shall be, we must certainly admit that the position of the wife in the household is that of subjection.

Turning to the Bible, and repeating our inquiry, we find what seems to be a confirmation of the verdict of history. Of course the Scripture gives no countenance to the barbaric notion that the wife is the property of her husband, that he may wreak his passion upon her, or repudiate her at his pleasure; but the doctrine seems to be taught, that woman is in a subordinate if not in a subject condition; that the authority and power belong to the husband.

The record of the creation gives no hint of any

superiority of one above the other, save as the man was created first. But this proves nothing at all, or else too much for advocates of masculine supremacy, since the other animals were created before man; and if priority of creation be the ground of eminence, they are higher in the scale than he. The curse that followed the fall seems to have rested upon woman more heavily than upon man; and it is mentioned as one of the evil incidents of her fallen state, that her desire shall be unto the man, and he shall rule over her. But it would seem that the condition into which the fall brought human beings is precisely the condition in which they ought not to remain. This sentence in the curse is the prophecy of a fact, not the announcement of a law. The prophecy has been fulfilled, but the fact is not therefore justified. It is of course the law, that, when man is alienated from God, physical force instead of moral influence becomes the arbiter of his affairs. Woman is physically weaker than man, and therefore must be, while the race is in this condition, subject to him.

So far, then, as Genesis is concerned, I do not know that there is any indication that the normal condition of woman in the household is subject or even subordinate. The fact is foretold, that this should be her condition; the fulfilment of this prediction we have found in history. But it is also distinctly declared that the subjection is part of the misery of the fall, and this it is the aim of Christianity to remove.

I do not remember that this question of the relation of the sexes is definitely touched again until we come to the epistles. There is no word of Christ himself that favors the subjection of woman; but in the epistles of Paul and Peter there are certain advices that seem to bear this interpretation. The position of woman, both in the church and in the family, seems by their teachings to be that of subordination.

For instance, Paul says that woman must keep silence in the churches, that it is a shame for them to speak in the church. Many persons regard this as a rule to be universally observed; but a little study of the subject makes it probable that it refers to circumstances then existing at the East. The customs of society were such, that for a woman to take public part in any religious service would have been absolutely shocking. No Christian woman could have done such a thing without injuring her good name, and Paul's counsel is grounded on this fact  He does not want them to bring scandal upon themselves and the gospel they profess, by disregarding social customs and proprieties in this way.

For the same reason, Paul forbids women to appear in public assemblies without being closely veiled. It was then, and still is in the East, considered immodest for a woman to let her face be seen in public; and Paul exhorted Christian women to conform to that custom. If one command is binding on the women of to-day, the other is. If it is a shame for American women to speak in church, because Paul says so, it is equally a shame to permit their faces to be seen in church, or in the street, because Paul says so. If the one command has reference to the peculiar customs of society in the East, so does the other.

Now, it is, to say the least, quite possible that those passages in these epistles in which woman's position in the family is represented as subordinate may be interpreted in the same way. When Paul and Peter tell wives to be subject to their husbands, their advice may be founded upon the peculiarities of Oriental society rather than upon any unalterable law of the divine administration. Things being as they were, it might have been better that women should patiently endure the limitations of their lot than that they should attempt any sudden and violent revolution in society. The expectation may be, with regard to the condition of women in the family, as with regard to the condition of slaves in the state, that Christianity will gradually loosen their bonds, and make their social subjection impossible. Indeed, the time is prophesied when there shall be neither Jew nor Greek, neither bond nor free, *neither male nor female*, but all shall be one in Christ. Of course, this can only mean the abolition of the social disparity between the sexes. In patient waiting for the coming of that time, wives as well as slaves may be admonished to abide in that calling wherein they are called.

Such would seem to be the Scriptural teaching upon this subject. The whole tendency of Christianity is to relieve woman of the curse and misery of our fallen state. And if this supremacy of man and this subjection of woman are, as they are said to be in Genesis, part of the curse, then we ought to expect that they will gradually disappear; and that, as in the beginning, they twain shall be one flesh, with no hint of authority or precedence on the part of either.

The ideally perfect marriage then, is, that in which the whole mind and heart and will of husband and wife are perfectly united; in which their purposes, sympathies, desires, activities, perfectly blend. Perfect marriage requires the entire agreement of two equal and consenting wills; not the merging of one will in the other ; not authority on one side and submission on the other: but the perfect union of two who, though different, are in all respects equal.

I am quite aware that there are but few ideal marriages, as there are few ideal schools or churches or governments; and yet it is of the highest importance that we recognize the ideal, and come as near to the realization of it as we can.

But the old question comes up again in another shape: Suppose this perfect harmony does not exist between husband and wife, what then? Must not one or the other have power to decide in cases of disagreement, and must it not be understood *which* one? By no means. Two equal partners in business may disagree, will certainly disagree, from time to time, about their transactions: is power therefore given to one of them to decide in all cases of disagreement? Of course, no man would ever enter into partnership with the understanding that in all such cases he was to submit. Yet men contrive to live together in this relation for many years, each possessing equal powers with the other, and the two composing their differences, as they arise, in a spirit of harmony; sometimes one yielding, and sometimes the other. Usually in such a case there is a division of labor and responsibility; the one taking one department of the business, and the other another department, and each in his own department having the controlling voice. Something like this might be done in the family. At all events, I am convinced

8

that the less we have of authority on one side, and submission on the other, in the marriage relation, the happier we shall all be in that relation; that the agreement of equals is much better for both than mastership for the one and servantship for the other, even though the rule of the master may be just and kind, and the obedience of the servant free and willing.

Of course, absolutism is better than anarchy in the family as in the state; but the perfect law of liberty is far better than either.

Therefore I trust that in your family life this may be the idea recognized and striven after. I hope you will remember that in the Christian family the rights of the husband and the wife are exactly equal; that the one has no more right to dictate and denounce than the other. Authority and subjection are terms of the curse, which ought, after nineteen centuries of Christianity, to disappear from the vocabulary of wedlock.

I have reasons for believing that the tyrants do not all sit upon thrones. There are husbands and fathers who rule their households with a rod of iron: enforcing their mandates upon wives and children, if not with violence, at least with imperious sternness, keeping the whole family in awe of their despotic authority. There are men who seem to think that

their wives have no opinions, no tastes, no wishes, no
rights, that they are bound to respect; that it is only
for their royal selves, — to serve their needs, to
gratify their desires, to minister to their pleasure, —
that the family was ordained. This sacred relation is
outrageously profaned and abused when such a spirit
dwells in the one who calls himself the master of the
house.

I do not wish to be understood as suggesting, however, that there are no faults on the other side of the
house. If there are tyrants among men, there are
scolds among women. The unhappiness of the family
relation is not due to the one sex more than to the
other. The wrongs that women suffer at the hands
of men have been pretty fully set forth of late, and
I have no disposition to overlook them; but if the
men were to get up a series of conventions setting
forth the evils under which they are suffering, — the
extravagance, the frivolity, the indolence, the exasperating pettishness, that afflict them and try their
souls, — they might make a pretty strong representation. But that such a course of action would be
very foolish and injurious to themselves, as well as to
the other sex, appears to me very plain. The effect
of setting the two sexes against each other in battle
array, of hurling reproaches and recriminations from
the one side to the other, of reciting and magnifying

the wrongs done by one to the other, is and must be evil and only evil. You cannot mend matters of this sort by public meetings. They will not make husbands any less tyrannical, I am sure; and I doubt whether they will make wives any more amiable. You cannot reform and elevate the family by blowing a breeze of political agitation over the land, any more than you can cure disease by statute and proclamation. The remedy for the disorders of the household must come from other sources. By the recognition of a higher ideal, by the growth of a purer Christianity, by the faithful and patient effort of both husbands and wives to help and serve each other in this relation, by ceasing to quarrel about rights, and thinking more of the privileges, the opportunities, the blessings of the family, — by such means as these, the mischiefs of the home will be most surely mended, and the best welfare secured.

But I must make haste to add one word concerning the ruling of the household, as it affects the children. In their earliest years, they are utterly helpless and dependent; and this fact gives to their parents authority over them. The relation between the parents, which is that of equals, is wholly different from that of the parent to the child, which is that of ruler and subject. The parents have not only a right, but it is their duty, to govern their children.

The ignorance and inexperience of the children
makes it their duty. It is my duty to restrain my
child from thrusting his hand into the fire, or from
throwing himself down the staircase, in his infancy ;
and it is equally my duty, when he grows a little
older, to keep him from evil society and bad books
and hurtful habits. It is my duty to train him up in
ways of industry and prudence and honesty. He will
not of his own accord enter these ways; and for
the sake of his future, I must lead him into them.
Knowing better than he does what is good for him,
what course he ought to take in childhood to reach a
virtuous and prosperous manhood, it is my duty to
guide him in that course, even though he may be
strongly inclined to walk in another direction.

But, while the exercise of a firm and just authority
by parents over their children is always necessary,
yet the fact must always be kept in mind, that these
children are by and by to pass out from under the
authority of their parents into freedom. The business of the parents is therefore to train them for the
liberty with which they are soon to be intrusted. It
is our duty to care for our children in such a way
that they shall be enabled shortly to care for themselves ; to govern them in such a way that they shall
be able, on coming to their majority, to govern
themselves. This involves the steady enlargement

of the liberty of the child, from the moment when he begins to use his reason. Children learn to walk by walking, to talk by talking, to sing by singing; and they can learn in no other way. Many tumbles on the floor, many blunders in orthoepy and syntax, many false notes in music, are certain incidents of their progress. If they are allowed to make no mistakes they will make no progress. So with their moral training. There must be government, but there must not be despotism. Some liberty of choice must be allowed to them, and they must be taught to use their liberty. They must be counselled, warned, guided; if need be, restrained; but no more authority should be used than is absolutely necessary. "Because I say so," is the very last reason to give for a command or a prohibition. " Because it is right " or " wise," these are the reasons which ought to be most used in directing the child's action. Reason and love are commonly more potent than autocratic will, in securing a cheerful obedience.

I can sum up all that has been said about the ruling of the household, by saying that the rights of the husband and the wife are exactly equal ; each has a right to claim from the other respect, sympathy, and affection ; that the rights of parents and children are reciprocal, the children having a right to the care of their parents, and to just such a measure of liberty for themselves at every stage of their development as they can safely and profitably use; and the parents having the right, within these limits, to the deference and obedience of their children. If the husband treats his wife as though she were his inferior, as though her opinion were not just as much to be regarded, her will just as much to be respected as his own in family affairs, the wife is wronged. If the wife by her extravagance, her inefficiency, her petulance, embarrasses and annoys her husband, he is wronged. If the parents neglect their children, or indulge them too freely, or tyrannize over them too sternly, the children are wronged. If the children refuse to their parents the honor and obedience that are their due, the parents are wronged. But too much talk of rights and wrongs is pernicious. This is the letter that killeth, but there is a spirit that giveth life. In the family, as under the divine government, love is the fulfilling of the law. A true and deep affection solves all these questions of obligation. Wherever it exists, there is no more dispute about rights, no more complaint of wrongs. The deference of the husband, the homage of the wife, the authority of the parents, the obedience of the children, are no more cold, severe, mechanical, but luminous and beautiful with heavenly light and grace.

The sacredness of the family relation, the ends it is designed to accomplish in restraining from sin and in leading to virtue, the conditions upon which it is happily founded and wisely ruled, have thus passed before our minds in rapid review. I do not know that what has been said has any more application to one class of persons than to another; but I have addressed these words to the working people, because I know that when the home is happy the labor is always light. The thought of the love and cheer awaiting him when his day's work is done takes the sting from the workman's toil. And I could think of no better service that I could hope to render him, than to show him, as well as I could, the foundations upon which the happiness of his home could be most securely built.

# VI.

## SOCIETY AND SOCIETIES.

IN civilized communities, men associate themselves for various purposes. The greater part of the world's work is done by associated effort. Not only does combination result in greater efficiency of labor, but it is pleasanter for the workmen to labor in company than to labor alone. A great part of the bitterness and burden of toil is removed by the fellowship of labor. When I was a farmer's boy I found it hard to work alone. The farm-work was not particularly distasteful to me if there was anybody to work with; even the company of a team of horses was better than none: but to go away by myself in a lonely field, and work all day, cutting down sprouts or picking up stones, with nobody to talk with, — that was tedious business. And I suspect that the thing which draws so many boys from the farms to the towns is, more than any thing else, the love of society. Men work together, therefore, not only because it is more profitable, but because it is, as a rule, more agreeable.

For purposes of education they are also associated. To this result we find the same double motive of interest and pleasure contributing. Economy of labor is not the only reason for gathering students into schools: they generally learn more rapidly in school than at home; they inspire and stimulate one another; and they enjoy the association. The sports and the friendships of the schools afford most of them an enjoyment that greatly lightens the labor required of them.

Benevolence, too, brings men together. There are societies for the promotion of temperance, and societies for the relief of suffering; and societies, commonly secret, for mutual assistance and protection. Doubtless desire to do good leads many to unite with such societies; doubtless others join them in the hope of getting some selfish advantage from them: but the social opportunity they offer is one strong attraction by which they recruit their ranks.

For purposes of entertainment, society is sought. The lecture, the concert, the oratorio, the opera, the drama, are offered always to assemblages of people.

This is not only because the expense of such enter-tainments is lightened by dividing it among a large number of people, but because the pleasure derived from them is greatly enhanced by enjoying them in company. Not only is it generally impossible for an orator or a singer to speak or sing well without the inspiration of numbers; it is equally impossible for an auditor to hear well without the same inspiration. If the performance in the presence of a single person were in every respect as good as in the crowded hall. his enjoyment of it would be greatly lessened by the want of company.

The same principle holds good in our religious life. The churches as well as the workshops, the schools, and the secret lodges, are organized under this law. Three objects are sought in the churches, — worship, instruction, and benevolent activity. It is true that one may worship alone acceptably; but it is also true that this highest act of the soul is sometimes made more delightful and more profitable by companion-ship. Praise is one chief element of worship; and, though one may sing praises to God alone, how much is added to the fervor and enthusiasm of our singing when we join with the great congregation! Prayer is the other act of worship; and while secret prayer is indispensable to the maintenance of the spiritual life, the helps of social prayer are also indispensable.

So far as instruction is provided by our churches, might not that be gained without association? Might we not read our Bibles and our religious books at home? and would not the instruction thus obtained be, on the whole, more complete and more valuable than that which we get from the pulpit? Throughout Christendom, every Sunday, much good preaching is heard, along with some that would be called indifferent, and not a little that must be pronounced very poor; but the members of these congregations could, at a trifling expense, have provided themselves with printed sermons of a high order. Why would it not be better, so far as religious instruction is concerned, if the people of our congregations should stay at home on Sundays and read good sermons, instead of going to church to hear in many cases indifferent or poor ones? The common answer to this question is, that the truth uttered by the living voice is more impressive than that read out of a book; that a poor sermon spoken is more effective upon the average man than a good sermon read. There is truth in this answer, but it is not the whole truth. The reason why it is better for people to receive instruction in the congregation than to study privately is, that the congregation is itself a stimulus not only to the preacher, but to every auditor. The mind of every hearer is quickened, his emotions are aroused, his better nature is warmed into life, by the influence of the assembly. It is not the living voice, so much as the living audience, that makes a tolerable sermon heard from the pulpit more impressive than a better sermon read from the book in the closet.

In the great work of benevolent activity, as in every other work, the same principle applies. It is easier and pleasanter to do good in company than alone. Not only by combination and division of labor is the work lightened and facilitated, but the enthusiasm and *esprit de corps* that spring up in the body of workers are a great help in the work.

We have seen that the social principle enters into nearly every department of human life, infusing itself through our work, our study, our play, our charity, our religion. And not only does this element control every phase of life: it creates a department of its own. Everywhere we find people associating, not for such purposes as we have named, but for the sake of society. There are assemblages called together simply for social purposes. In the rural districts, we see the housewives gathering with their knitting-work at one of the neighbors' houses for an afternoon chat and a social cup of tea, and the young rustics assembling from time to time in the evening, to engage in merry games. In the villages and the cities, the social life finds expression in many ways that I need not describe; some of which are good, and others of which are mingled with much evil.

So constant and universal are the social forces in the life of human beings, that the race as a whole is often spoken of as society. The attraction that binds men together in society is apparently stronger than any other principle of human nature. It becomes, then, an important question, what our relations to society should be; how these all-pervading influences shall affect our lives.

The design of the Creator was, that every one of his creatures should have a character of his own. One of the ends most plainly sought by him is the individuality of each distinct existence. No two faces are alike, we often say; and it is equally true that no two minds are alike: tastes and preferences vary indefinitely. Now, it is of the utmost importance that this individuality be preserved and cherished. A landscape is not beautiful because the objects it shows us are all alike, but because they are all different, yet are harmoniously grouped and blended in the view. An art-gallery interests us, and is of value to its owner, not because the paintings or the statues are all alike, but because each is a different representation of beauty. Five hundred copies of the

Sistine Madonna arranged in rows upon the wall of the academy would offend us. Iteration is wearisome, no matter how beautiful the expression may be. Would you like to read a book that consisted of an endless repetition of a single sentence? What nature would be if all its objects were cast in one mould, what art would be if it were only the monotonous repetition of the same forms and colors, what literature would be if it were the ceaseless recurrence of the same words in the same order, — that would society be if all men were alike. When each man is permitted to develop his own individuality, the intellectual wealth of society is increased; but when this individuality is repressed, when men are made to conform to certain fixed standards of thought and custom, society is impoverished. Yet the tendency is very strong, in all states of society, to repress individuality.

Of course it is a necessary condition of society, that individuals shall conform in some respects to the wishes of their fellows. Men cannot associate in business without self-denial, without subordinating their views and preferences in certain particulars to those of others. An utter wilfulness, an obstinate, perverse disposition, is destructive of society. It becomes, therefore, an important question for every one of us, just how far we ought to govern ourselves by social laws and customs, and how far we ought to manifest the life that is in us in our own way.

Society, in all circles, is quite peremptory in its demands. It lays down certain laws of behavior; it prescribes certain styles of dress; it has fashions in every thing. There are books that it is fashionable to read, and dishes that it is fashionable to eat, and churches that it is fashionable to attend, and stores that it is fashionable to patronize, and opinions that it is fashionable to hold; and society is rather inclined to be intolerant of those who will not follow all its fashions. There are social customs that we may safely and profitably follow. To disregard them all, to place ourselves outside of society, and make war upon it, is almost as bad as to be its bond-servant. One may err in setting his will against society in trifling matters. There are requirements of custom that in themselves are neither right nor wrong: they involve no moral principle whatever: it is as easy to conform to them as not; and to stand out about such small things belittles the mind.

It is clear, however, that society has no right to interfere with our opinions of truth, with our convictions of duty. Every one of us must give account for himself to God. Every one of us ought to be fully persuaded in his own mind of the rightfulness of any practice in which moral principle is involved. The attempt to enforce upon individuals conventional notions of truth and duty, right and wrong, is both absurd and wicked. Of course, there is one limit to the liberty of individuals, even in this direction. No man may be permitted to injure his fellow-men for conscience' sake. But in cases where his conduct affects nobody but himself, each man must be allowed to decide for himself; and any attempt on the part of society to prescribe his opinions, or rule his practices, is mischievous in the extreme.

The problem we are considering is not easily solved, but it is very easily stated. In society, as in every other organized existence, beauty and perfection are secured by unity in variety, the harmonious combination of parts that differ. To secure the unity that is necessary, it is needful that there should be some conformity to social standards and usages. To secure the variety that is desirable, it is well that the individuality of every man and woman be perfectly developed. It is necessary, therefore, to learn how to reconcile these two contending obligations; how to be in society, and not of it; how to respect yourself, your own judgment and conscience, and yet to love your neighbor as yourself; when to withstand the social influences, and when to yield to them. It is not always easy to tell in such a case

9

what we ought to do; but it is useful to know what the elements are that enter into the problem.

The law of social intercourse is, of course, the law of love. The charity that envieth not, that seeketh not her own, that is not easily provoked, that thinketh no evil, is the only trait that can qualify any one to make the right use of society. No profitable social intercourse can ever take place between persons that are more eager to receive than to confer favor and honor. A true self-forgetfulness, a sincere desire to make others happy, is the essential qualification for social life. The best gifts avail nothing to one who is lacking in this. In the various social organizations, there are those who want the offices and the conspicuous places, and are sour and cross if they cannot get them. Among associations of musicians, I have heard it alleged that some are always taking offence if leading parts are not assigned them. In the churches, people have been known to complain because not enough notice was taken of them. Those who never in their lives were suspected of making the slightest effort to increase the welfare or the happiness of their neighbors, often grumble because their neighbors are not more diligent in seeking them out and showing them kindness. Such a spirit as this makes society impossible.

Individuality, tractableness, charity, — these are

the three elements of the best social life. In our intercourse with our fellows, it is of the utmost importance that we stand firmly by our own convictions of truth and duty, that we be easily entreated in things indifferent, and that we govern all our conduct by the law of Christian love.

The family life of working-people, of which I wrote in the preceding chapter, does not greatly differ in its obligations or its privileges from that of other people; but the social life of mechanics and laborers is, in certain important respects, unlike that of the wealthier classes; and I desire to speak now, briefly, of society as it offers itself to working-men and working-women.

1. The social relations of working-people in their work may be of great advantage to them. Among shopmates, a deep and lasting friendship often springs up. You cannot always pick your company in your work, but you can hardly be so unfortunate as not to find much that is pleasant and helpful. Because your opportunities of society outside of your labor are by the necessities of the case somewhat limited, you ought to make the most of these friendships with your workfellows, and to derive all the benefit you can from your association with them.

2. It will be wise, however, for you to seek for

opportunities of social intercourse in your leisure hours. For your own good, and for the good of the community, you ought to bear your part in the development of social life  It does a man good, who works hard all day at some disagreeable employment, to put on clean raiment of an evening, and go out into good company. The refining influence thus exerted upon him he cannot safely forego.

It is not only for the sake of his manners that he needs this social culture, but for the sake of his morals as well. Workday life is full of rivalries and competitions, of cheating and over-reaching, of an endless suppressed warfare among men. " Every man for himself," is the maxim of traffic; and every man is obliged to look out for himself, or he will be fleeced and ruined. This is done for the most part in lawful and polite and even obsequious ways, but it is done. No matter what station of life you are in, there is need of constant vigilance to secure your rights. Of course when you go home, if you have a home, you pass out of this arena of strife and competition into a different atmosphere, where nobody is trying to get the advantage of you; where the law of love rules instead of the law of competition. And it is one of the greatest blessings a home gives us, that it affords us such a refuge from the angry contests of the world. But it is good for us also to feel

that this spirit of good-will and mutual kindness prevails outside of our homes. And the supposition is,
that our social life is controlled by this spirit. It is
true that jealousies and envyings and rivalries do
find their way into society; but the theory is, and to
a great extent it is the practice too, that good-will
and kindness prevail in social circles. Therefore it
is good for us all to escape from the clash and clamor
of business now and then, and meet our fellows, not
on a footing of rivalry, but on a footing of friendli-
ness: to exercise ourselves, not in getting the advantage of them, nor in guarding ourselves against their
attempts to get the advantage of us, but in showing
them respect and polite attention. If Scrooge meets
his neighbor in a friendly way at a sociable, he will
be a little less likely to gouge him the next day in
a bargain. The enmities that spring up between
neighbors are often prevented or healed by bringing them together socially. It seems to me, that if
it were not for these occasional opportunities of
friendly intercourse, — these assemblies that have no
other purpose than to foster the social sentiments,
— we should ere long relapse into barbarism. It is
impossible to exaggerate the humanizing and ameliorating influence exerted by them upon the rough and
bitter life through which we are daily passing.

3. The methods of diversion with which you shall

fill up your social hours, you must choose for yourselves. You are often invited to evening parties
more or less public, some of which are conducted in
such a way as to be entirely unobjectionable, and
some of which are not. The mischief of such assemblies is in the excesses to which they lead, and the
late hours to which they are frequently protracted.
Many of your parties are dancing parties. I have
never been able to believe that it is a sin to dance;
but it is true that it is a pastime more liable to abuse
than many others, and that you can hardly guard too
carefully against the evils that grow out of it. As it
is wholly a muscular exercise, I should doubt its usefulness as a frequent recreation for persons whose
work is nearly all muscular. Some lighter and
quieter enjoyment would be preferable, — something
that would divert the mind without further fatiguing
the body. Diversions that bring you into the
society of corrupt companions, or that overtax your
strength, are always pernicious.

Public shows and performances often invite you,
promising to gratify at once the love of recreation
and the love of society, — two passions of human
nature that are distinct, but hardly ever separate. I
should be far from condemning these exhibitions by
wholesale. It is necessary, I suppose, that the people
should have diversions provided for them; and some

of these travelling shows are probably innocent and good enough. In general it may be said, first, that performances in which either immorality or indelicacy is even so much as suggested, ought to be shunned. Never attend any place of amusement in which you would not be glad to have your mother or your sister sitting by your side. In the second place, only a limited amount of this sort of diversion is wholesome. The habit that some working-people have of running to all the shows that come to town is a very bad habit. It costs a good deal, for one thing. The money that is spent in this way by some families would, if saved and invested, provide them with homes in a few years. I knew one family that actually stripped their beds of the clothing that made them comfortable, and sold it, to get money to attend a circus. By far the largest part of the money that is carried out of this city every year by the travelling exhibitions (and that is no small sum) comes from the pockets of the working-people. I heard one carpenter tell another, a few days ago, that he had attended every circus that had been in the city this year. He did not speak of it as if his case was an exceptional one, and I do not suppose that it was. Surely a better use could have been found for part of the money thus expended.

But the effect upon the mind, of such a constant

attendance upon these extravagant performances, is worse than the effect upon the purse  I knew a young mechanic in New York who attended the negro-minstrel entertainments so constantly that he came to live and move and have his being in the atmosphere of burnt cork. You could not talk with him ten minutes without finding out his penchant. The grotesque manners, the absurd expressions, the exaggerated notions, that characterize their performances, were continually appearing in his conduct and conversation. He seemed to be saturated with negro-minstrelsy, and it oozed out at every pore. What a condition of mind that must be, I leave you to imagine. Individuals outside of New York have been seen in a similar state. The dissipating, enfeebling effect upon the mind and the moral nature of frequent attendance upon these farcical and sensational performances is pitiful indeed. Working-people need diversion, and I would not be too fastidious in my criticism of their methods of seeking it; but it seems to me that many of them would find more solid enjoyment by cultivating their tastes for a higher order of amusements, such as good literary or scientific lectures, fine concerts, and poetic readings. The taste for these more elevated recreations can be acquired; and instead of debilitating the mind, they give it refreshment and wholesome stimulus.

I come now to speak briefly of those organizations formed by working-men, partly for social purposes, and partly for the improvement of their circumstances. In almost all trades such societies are found. They have grown out of the conflict between labor and capital, and are intended mainly for offensive and defensive warfare. The attempt has also been made to unite the guilds that represent the various trades in one great national labor organization, so that a concerted movement may be made at any time, by the whole body of workmen, to secure higher rates of wages.

So far as the work of these societies is of a social character, no fault can be found with it. Workingmen may promote, by association, their own knowledge and enjoyment. They may also assist one another to find employment, care for one another in sickness, shield one another from temptation. Such efforts are worthy of all commendation.

Besides this, they may wish to consult about their own interests; and if they do this soberly and peaceably, no fault can be found. They have a perfect right to deliberate together concerning the wages they are receiving, and to unite in refusing to work unless their wages are increased. The law gives to capital an immense advantage in permitting its consolidation in great centralized corporations;

and neither law nor justice can forbid laborers to combine, in order to protect themselves against the encroachments of capital, so long as they abstain from the use of violence, and rely upon reason and moral influence.

But it needs no prophet to tell that these societies are liable to become instruments of evil as well as of good. It happens that a large proportion of the members of most of them are ignorant men, whose passions are easily excited, and who may be led to take very fanatical and absurd views of the labor question. And whenever any large number of such men are brought into company, the devil, in the form of the demagogue or the charlatan, comes also among them. It makes one sick and sad to see the kind of leaders to whom the workmen in these societies often intrust the management of their affairs, — noisy, crazy, crack-brained creatures, whose capital stock of political philosophy consists of one or two half-truths, and a full assortment of lies. To hear these blatherskites talk, to read the dreadful stuff that they write, and then to think that they are the chosen representatives of the working-people, is very discouraging. We have in this Commonwealth a few such persons, who have been prominent in the councils of the labor leagues, and whose nostrums have been freely vended in the shape of tracts among the working-men. They are always opposed to any peaceful solution of the labor question: they want to win by revolution, or not at all. Their creed is simply a dilution of the doctrines of Proudhon, whose works they are printing and distributing, and whose fundamental maxim is, that property is robbery. Of course intelligent American mechanics, who have been educated in our common schools, know too much to be imposed upon by such nonsense; and quickly refuse to follow such a lead. A large number of those who constitute these associations, however, are *not* intelligent American mechanics; and therefore the fanatics often get control of them, and contrive to shape their policy.

Men in masses often do very strange things. This is true not only of working-men, but of all sorts of men. When I was in college, I know that we used to do some things as a class, or as a college, that few of the students would have done if they had been alone. It is sometimes said, that in a multitude of counsellors there is wisdom; but that depends on the kind of counsellors. A thousand wise men may be wiser than one wise man; but it by no means follows that a thousand fools are wiser than one fool: on the contrary, they may be a thousand times as foolish. Those Roman bishops that formed the Vatican council egged one another on to the almost unanimous promulgation of a dogma which, if they had been questioned about it singly beforehand, the majority of them would have pronounced doubtful if not false. A crowd that contains many sensible men will sometimes do surprisingly silly things.

This is the danger against which these working-men's societies must always be on their guard. The mob spirit sometimes takes possession of the body, and no privilege of differing with the crowd is willingly allowed to any workman. If violence is not resorted to in the quieting of dissenters, there is a sort of social persecution not much better than violence. The person that refuses his assent to the measures resolved upon is denounced as a traitor; and a disposition is shown to make the place too hot for him. In such persecution no fair-minded man will join; to this intimidation no brave man will submit. Never sell out your manhood to any man, or set of men. Do not be bribed or coaxed or bullied into doing what you think is not right. Let nobody decide for you what is right. Make up your own mind, and stand by it, no matter what it costs.

These labor-unions have certain rules that cannot be defended on any principle of justice. They often forbid their members to work in company with non-union men, and force employers to discharge all such persons. They will not suffer a boy to learn their trade, unless his father belongs to their society. This is nothing but despotism, despotism of the most brutal sort: working-men ought to be ashamed to resort to it.

The leaders of these societies tell us it is necessary that they should combine, to resist the extortions of capitalists; and that their combinations will amount to nothing, unless there is firm discipline in their ranks. Yes, "discipline:" that was precisely what the lords of the lash on the Southern plantations used to call it; that is just what all the despots that have ever trampled on the liberties of men have always called it. The word sounds well; but sometimes, when most sweetly spoken, it means tyranny. And I say that any man of proper spirit will be careful how he puts his neck into the yoke of this "discipline;" and will resist unto blood, rather than suffer it to be bound upon him by any power whatsoever.

Heaven forbid that I should lay a straw in the way of working-men engaged in any just attempt to improve their condition! I know something of their lot: as farmer's boy and as mechanic's apprentice, I have entered pretty fully into their life, and tasted something of its severities, and something, also, of the independence and manly dignity with which it may always be clothed; and it is just because all my sympathies are with working-men, that I want to see them abstain from questionable and suicidal methods. ⌈They will never prosper by violence or injustice : light and liberty are their only true allies.⌋

I have left myself but little time to speak of one other social organization in which working-people ought to take a deep interest : I meàn the Christian Church. Already I have more than once expressed to you my sense of the relation between the religion of Christ and your welfare. I think you have seen pretty clearly that this religion has done more for you than any other instrumentality on earth, and that the light which touches your future with hope and promise is the light that breaks from the gospel of Christ.

Almost all the legitimate objects that you seek in your various social organizations, the Church, if rightly viewed by you, would aid you in securing. If companionship is what you want, the Church is the fraternity whose bond is closer and more sacred than any other; if you desire culture, you will find that most churches in these days recognize the fact that knowledge is one of the Christian graces, and strive to enrich the minds, as well as to purify the hearts, of their members; if you crave diversion, that too is provided for to a sufficient degree. For the Church must have it for its aim, to build up the whole man symmetrically, — to give every human faculty its appropriate nutriment, that " the man of God may be perfect and entire, wanting nothing." If you seek opportunity for benevolent work, I am safe in saying that more of this is done by the churches of the land than by all other organizations put together; if you wish to better your condition in a worldly point of view, your safest course is to study and practise those principles of Christian prudence and morality which it is the office of the Church to teach. I admit that the Church has its faults; that the principles on which it is founded are often but imperfectly apprehended by those who administer its affairs; that there is no little human nature within as well as without its communion : yet so long as the New Testament is its charter, so long as faith in the man of Nazareth and loyalty to him is its foundation, it must be a mighty power for good in the world. And I am sure that, if you have not already done so, you cannot find any thing better to do than to connect yourself with some Christian congregation, and take part in its work.

You may think that I am talking professionally now, but I am not. I go right back in my thought to the day when I was a mechanic's apprentice, alone and almost friendless in a large town; and I speak solely from my memory of the help, the solace, the stimulus, that a Christian church then gave me. I never think of that church, of the dear friendships to which it introduced me, of the quickening that it gave me mentally as well as spiritually, of the better purposes of living into which it led me, without the deepest thankfulness. It furnished just the kind of influence that I needed, at a critical time in my life ; and I owe to its sacred associations more than I shall ever be able to tell.

# VII.

## STRONG DRINK.

THE evils that result from the drinking of intoxicating liquors are not hidden from working-men. The statement that a large proportion of the pauperism and crime of the land is directly traceable to strong drink, is one that their observation will verify. Rum builds and fills our prisons and our almshouses; rum greatly increases the burden of our taxation.

The secretary of the Massachusetts Board of State Charities lately reported that " from three-fourths to four-fifths of the crime for which persons are inmates of the House of Correction and the prison may be traced to intemperance. In the almshouse perhaps four-fifths of the inmates are brought there by intemperance. Some persons have estimated the

145

proportion as larger than that. Between five and six hundred persons are supported by the State in the insane asylum; and a large proportion of the cases of insanity may be traced to intemperance."

The testimony of the chaplain of the Charlestown prison is still stronger: " Since I have been there, I have conversed with over fourteen hundred different men; and I have spoken with them particularly with regard to the matter of intoxicating drinks; and, out of that number, fifteen-sixteenths have stated that liquor had something to do with their coming there."

Judge Sanger of Boston, a prosecuting attorney of Massachusetts, gives it as his opinion, that " a large portion of the criminal costs of the Commonwealth are from this cause. There are very few cases into which the use of intoxicating liquors does not more or less enter."

These witnesses being true, the testimony which they utter deserves our careful attention. For those who are not themselves addicted to the use of strong drink must suffer greatly in their pecuniary interests, and may suffer in their families, from the evils that intemperance brings into society. If any thing can be done to check its ravages, working-men are interested in having it done without delay.

The first thing to do is to reform the drinking customs of society. We cannot stop the sale of liquor by law till we get the great majority of the people to believe that it injures them to drink liquor. If we could induce all the people who drink to stop drinking, the people who sell would be obliged to stop selling. And if, by showing them its evil effects, we can persuade a large number of those who use strong drink to give it up, we can prepare a moral basis broad and firm enough for a stringent law.

To begin with, then, it is safe to say that the drinking of intoxicating liquors does no healthy person any good. Nearly all the doctors admit that they are valuable medicines in some diseases, and that they may be used with advantage in certain feeble and morbid states of the system; but the best authorities are pretty clear in their affirmation that, if a man is well, strong drink will not make him any better.

One of the effects of alcohol upon the system is to retard the waste of tissue. Those of you who have studied physiology a little, know that two processes are constantly going on in the healthy human body. The food we eat and the air we breathe are all the while adding to its substance; and other agencies are all the while eliminating the portions that are worn out. One set of forces is at work building up the tissues, and another set is at work pulling them down and carrying them off. It is necessary to health that both of these processes should go on at the same time: if one goes on without the other, disorder and disease are the result. Sometimes the body is in such a condition that the digestive and assimilative forces do not work well, and the others keep on wasting the tissues and diminishing the strength. The destroyers are at work, but the builders have stopped working. In such cases alcoholic liquors are sometimes useful because they prevent the waste of tissues; they simply make the destroyers stop working till the builders are ready to go on.

In cases of great weakness, the use of these liquors as medicines is undoubtedly beneficial. Dr. Bellows of Boston, testifying before a committee of the Legislature, uses these words: "Keeping in mind that the synonyme of stimulant is goad, I have no difficulty in coming to a conclusion when it is needful as a medicine. I have stood by the bedside of a sinking patient when the pulse was sinking rapidly, and when I have feared that nature would not be able to rally, and I have given a stimulant, — a goad to whip up poor sinking nature; and in a few moments the pulse would rise, but would fall again very soon. It might be carefully renewed till nature was able to receive some nourishment. I believe that patients have been saved by the use of stimulants in such a manner."

For purposes of this nature alcoholic liquors may, undoubtedly, be wisely used; and it is only in such cases that they are beneficial. The physician is the only person who can properly determine when they ought to be resorted to.

Concerning the habitual use of them as beverages by persons in health, I do not ask you to take my opinions, but quote for you the highest medical authority. Dr. Carpenter of England, who is perhaps the most distinguished physiologist in the world, makes this statement: "The physiological objection to the habitual use of even small quantities of alcoholic drinks rests upon the following grounds: They are universally admitted to possess a poisonous character; they tend to produce a morbid condition of the body at large; the capacity for enduring the extremes of heat and cold, or mental and bodily labor, is diminished rather than increased by their habitual employment. . . . Alcoholic liquids cannot supply any thing that is essential to the due nutrition of the system. The action of alcohol upon the living body is essentially that of stimulus, increasing for a time the vital activity of the body, but being followed by a corresponding depression of power, which is the more prolonged and severe as the previous excitement has been greater."

Sir Henry Thompson, one of the most eminent medical practitioners of England, who is best known in this country as Prof. Tyndall's friend, and the author of the "Prayer Gauge," testifies as follows: "I have long had the conviction that there is no greater cause of evil, moral and physical, in this country, than the use of alcoholic beverages. I do not mean by this that extreme indulgence which produces drunkenness. The habitual use of fermented liquors, to an extent far short of what is necessary to produce that condition, and such as is quite common in all ranks of society, injures the body, and diminishes the medical power, to an extent which I think few people are aware of. Such, at all events, is the result of observation during more than twenty years of professional life, devoted to hospital practice, and to private practice in every rank above it. Thus I have no hesitation in attributing a very large proportion of some of the most painful and dangerous maladies which come under my notice, as well as those which every medical man has to treat, to the ordinary and daily use of *fermented drink, taken in the quantity which is conventionally deemed· moderate.* Whatever may be said in regard to its evil influence on the mental and moral faculties, as to the fact above stated I feel that I have a right to speak with authority ; and I do so solely because it appears to me a duty, especially at this moment, not to be silent on a matter of such extreme importance. . . . My main object is to express my opinion, as a professional man, in relation to the habitual employment of fermented liquor as a beverage. But if I ventured one step further, it would be to express a belief that there is no single habit in this country which so much tends to deteriorate the qualities of the race, and so much disqualifies it for endurance in that competition which, in the nature of things, must exist, and in which struggle the prize of superiority must fall to the best and the strongest."

Sir Henry Thompson is not a fanatic : he looks at this question from a scientific rather than a sentimental point of view; and his words will have weight with you for this reason. You will notice that his judgment includes fermented liquors. The theory of Gov. Andrew, that the habitual use of wine and beer is not only harmless but beneficial, is expressly contradicted by this high authority.

In England, as is well known, total abstinence is not practised among the higher classes of society so generally as it is in this country. Wine is commonly found at the ministers' meetings: Mr. Spurgeon uses it freely, and justifies this use of it. There has been, till recently, no public sentiment averse to moderate drinking. But of late our English cousins, who are slow in changing their views of such subjects, have been investigating the physiological effects of alcoholic liquors much more thoroughly than we have ever done. During the last few years, "The British Medical Journal" has invited contributions from those best qualified to speak upon the subject; and Dr. Markham, the distinguished editor of this journal, thus sums up the results of the discussion which has appeared upon its pages: —

"We have no wish hastily to speak on this important matter; but we are bound in conscience boldly to declare the logical and inevitable conclusions, as they seem to us, to which a scientific view of the subject forces us.

"1. That alcohol is not food, and that, being simply a stimulant of the nervous system, its use is hurtful to the body of a healthy man.

"2. That if its imbibition be of service, it is only so to man in an abnormal condition, and that our duty as men of medicine is to endeavor to define what those particular abnormal states are in which alcohol is serviceable.

"3. That ordinary social indulgence in alcoholic drinks for society's sake is, medically speaking, a very unphysiological and prejudicial proceeding."

American authorities of equal eminence might be quoted to the same effect. A statement of Dr. Willard Parker, is every whit as strong as that of Sir Henry Thompson.

Such are some of the opinions of scientific men upon this subject. The doctors do not agree about it, of course : there are very few subjects on which they do agree; but the men to whom I have referred you stand very high in their profession, and their testimony fully sustains the statement with which we started, that the use of strong drink does no healthy person any good. As scientific men, their opinions are based upon facts which they have observed and collated ; and I now desire to call your attention to some of these facts, that you may judge for yourselves whether the opinions that I have quoted have a sufficient foundation.

It is maintained by drinkers, that their strength and their endurance are increased by the moderate use of alcoholic beverages. Facts prove, however, that the strength and endurance of human beings are greatly diminished by the use of such beverages.

In forming our judgment on this point, it is necessary, of course, to make a wide induction of facts. You can quote to me instances of individual drinkers who have lived to a great age, and who have performed much labor, and endured many hardships ; but concerning all such cases I should ask you two questions: First, are you sure that they are not exceptions to a general rule? Second, how do you know they would not have lived longer, done more work, and endured more hardships, if they had abstained from strong drink? A single fact is not enough to establish a scientific law. You must have a wide knowledge of facts bearing upon the case, and your verdict must be in accordance with the weight of evidence. Attempts have been made to reach certainty in this matter, by a careful collation of facts.

A gentleman in Uxbridge, Eng., kept account for a whole year of the work done by two gangs of brickmakers, one of which was composed of beer-drinkers, the other of total abstainers. Here is the result: "Out of upwards of 23,000,000 of bricks made in 1841 by the largest maker in the neighborhood, the average per man made by the beer-drinkers was 760,269; while the average for the teetotallers was 795,400, which is 35,131 in favor of the latter. The highest number made by a beer-drinker was 880,000; the highest number made by a teetotaller was 890,000, leaving ten thousand in favor of the teetotaller. The lowest number made by a beer-drinker was 659,000; the lowest number made by a teetotaller was 746,000, leaving 87,000 in favor of the teetotaller."

From another group of workers in a very different

field, we get the same testimony. The late Richard Cobden, speaking on one occasion of the severe labors of the parliament that debated the corn-laws, mentions that, out of 658 members, two gentlemen, Col. Thompson and Mr. Brotherton, endured the long sittings and wearisome debates of that body with greater ease than any other members, and they were both total abstainers.

I have no statistics to present with reference to the soldiers in the late war; but considerable observation of their habits, and inquiry among them, satisfied me that the fatigues of the hard marches were best borne by men who never tasted intoxicating liquors. A single witness will not prove the case, as I have admitted; but a witness whose testimony contradicts his inclinations has some special claims upon our credit. One of the best and bravest of the young officers of the Army of the Potomac, who was not during the war, and is not now, a total abstainer, was justifying, in a conversation with me, his use of strong drink. He drank it, he said, because he liked it; and that was reason enough. "But did you use it in the army?" I asked. "I did," he answered, "except on the heavy marches. Then I never touched a drop of whiskey. I found that it would not do. The men who stimulated always played out sooner than the men who abstained."

In another quarter we find an accumulation of weighty evidence. That is the testimony of the athletes, the oarsmen, the pugilists, the ball-players, the pedestrians, all the men who have made it the study and the business of their lives to secure the most perfect muscular development, from the days of the Olympic races down to the present time. Their testimony is very nearly uniform, that the highest degree of physical strength is impossible to one who drinks even moderately. The trainers of these athletes have always insisted that their men shall abstain from even the mildest forms of alcoholic liquors.

The literature of the ancients is full of references to the abstemious practices of the athletes. Thus Epictetus says, " Do you wish to gain the prize at the Olympic games? Consider the requisite preparations and the consequence. You must observe a strict regimen; . . . *you must take no wine as usual;* you must put yourself under a pugilist as under a physician, and afterward enter the lists." Thus Horace, as translated by Francis, bears witness in his essay on " The Art of Poetry : " —

> " A youth who hopes the Olympic prize to gain
> All arts must try, and every toil sustain;
> The extremes of heat and cold must often prove,
> And shun the weakening joys of wine and love."

A few of the trainers have lately attempted to
introduce beer into the regimen of the oarsmen; but
if I am rightly informed, the innovation has not been
successful. The experience of so many generations
in such a matter is not likely to lead us astray; and
it all helps to confirm the truth of the confession of
Tom Sayers: "I'm no teetotaller; but when I've any
business to do, there's nothing like water and the
dumb-bells."

One of the delusions most widely prevalent with
regard to alcoholic liquors is that they help to keep
the body warm. Liebig classes them among "respir-
atory foods," and maintains that they act, like fat and
similar substances, as fuel to increase the heat of the
body. Every habitual drinker will tell you that they
keep him warm on a cold day; and if you ask him
how he knows, he will tell you that he knows by his
feelings. So far as Liebig is concerned, his theory is
not now accepted by the highest authorities. Dr.
James C. White and Dr. Edward H. Clarke both
declared before the Massachusetts Legislative Committee, that it was "undemonstrated." And so far
as the drinker is concerned, it is sufficient to say that
the feelings are not always trustworthy guides. You
are not always warmest when you feel warmest. The
only safe guide is the thermometer. And if any man
will place the bulb of a thermometer in the current

of his breath or under his tongue, and note the temperature of his breath and of his blood before drinking a glass of brandy, and again a short time after drinking it, he will find that the temperature of his body is perceptibly lowered by the stimulant. Travellers in the Arctic regions report that the use of strong drink greatly lessens a man's power to endure hunger and cold and fatigue. Mr. Parton, in his essay entitled, "Will the Coming Man Drink Wine?" — an essay which has been of service to me in the preparation of this chapter, — relates the following on the authority of a traveller: "When Russian troops are about to start on a march in a very cold region, no grog is allowed to be served to them; and when the men are drawn up ready to move, the corporals smell the breath of every man, and send back to quarters all who have been drinking. The reason is that men who start under the influence of liquor are the first to succumb to the cold, and the likeliest to be frost-bitten. It is the uniform experience of the hunters and trappers of the northern provinces of North America and of the Rocky Mountains, that alcohol diminishes their power to resist cold."

Upon such facts as I have recited, scientific men rest their theory that strong drink is man's foe. The brick-maker, the law-maker, the soldier, the prizefighter, the pedestrian, the oarsman, the ball-player, the trapper, the arctic explorer, all unite in the testimony, that the man who wants to do his best must let alcoholic liquors entirely alone. Taken in ever so moderate quantities, they impair the strength of the body, and diminish its power of endurance.

Not only are they not friends to the health of man : they are also powerful allies of the diseases that prey upon him. When the dark shadow of pestilence falls upon any community, by far the largest proportion of its victims is found among those who make habitual use of stimulating beverages.

Dr. Cartwright, one of the best physicians of New Orleans, wrote thus to "The Boston Medical Journal" in 1853 : "The yellow fever came down like a storm upon this devoted city, with 1,127 dramshops in one out of four divisions of the city. It is not the citizens proper, but the foreigners, with their mistaken notions about the climate and the country, who are the chief supports of these haunts of intemperance. About five thousand of them died before the epidemic touched a single citizen or sober man, so far as I can get at the facts."

Dr. Bronson of Albany, who spent some time in Montreal during the prevalence of the cholera in 1852, wrote as follows: "Cholera has stood up here, as it has everywhere, the advocate of temperance. It has pleaded most eloquently, and with tremendous effect. The disease has searched the haunts of the drunkard, and has seldom left it without bearing away its victims. Even moderate drinkers have been but a little better off." Out of twelve hundred persons attacked by the cholera in Montreal during the summer of 1852, less than one hundred recovered; and one of the journals of the city stated that "almost all the victims were at least moderate drinkers."

The cholera and yellow fever proclaim with only a little louder voices the same truth that a hundred other sicknesses are telling us every day, — that strong drink is the forerunner, the armor-bearer, and the ally of all disease. More than once I have heard the physician tell his patient, on his recovery from a severe attack of pneumonia or typhoid fever, "If you had been a drinking man, you would never have come out of this." Even the moderate use of alcoholic beverages so impairs the vital energy of the system that it does not quickly rally from the shock of disease.

In the mortuary records we find a comparatively small number of deaths attributed to intemperance; but everybody knows that it is the efficient cause of thousands of deaths to which, to spare the feelings of sorrowing friends, the physicians assign other causes. Typhus fever and paralysis and peritonitis and heart disease, and numberless other ailments, are made the scapegoats of the mischief done by strong drink.

Thus we complete the circuit of our evidence. Life from every station and every calling, disease by every destroyer in its ghostly army, and death itself from every graveyard in the land, unite in the testimony that alcoholic liquors are the deadly foes of the human race, despoiling men of their strength, and joining hands with the dark slayer to do his terrible work.

Their effects upon the mental and moral nature are not less injurious. It is sometimes thought that the alertness and vigor of the mind are increased by the use of these stimulants; but it is not the fact. Dr. Brinton, a famous English physician, much quoted by Gov. Andrew in his speech against prohibition, says in his work on dietetics, "Mental acuteness, accuracy of perception, and delicacy of the senses, are all so far opposed by alcohol that the maximum efforts of each are incompatible with the ingestion of any moderate quantity of fermented liquid. A single glass will often serve to take the edge off both mind and body, and to reduce their capacity to something less than the perfection of work." This follows, as

11

an inevitable inference, from what has already been proven. For though the mind and the body are not identical, yet they are so closely related that whatever affects the one affects the other. The mind requires for its best working the best health of the body. But we have seen that even the moderate use of intoxicating liquors impairs the best health of the body, and therefore it must affect the mind injuriously.

The moral nature is part of the mind, and must therefore share in the injury. The effect of strong drink seems to be almost uniformly to stimulate the lower appetites and propensities, to aggravate the animalism of the nature, and to paralyze the nobler sentiments. It is well known that sensuality of the foulest type is nourished by ardent spirits. Go into any bar-room where a company of men are drinking together, and you will not stay long without hearing the vile jest or the indecent allusion. Lips that are clean in soberness are defiled when the intoxicating bowl touches them. The angel of purity flies from the place where drunken mirth holds wassail. And not only vile thoughts and vile words, but viler deeds, are the offspring of this demon. Intemperance is always the prime minister of lust. The saloon of the rumseller is next door to the house that is " the way of hell, going down to the chambers of death."

To every variety of crime, strong drink is the instigator. To the crime of arson, it very often prompts men. There is abundant evidence to show that the insane passion for burning — *pyromania*, as it is called — is often excited by it. Men who are perfectly free from such inclinations when sober are seized, when intoxicated, with an overpowering desire to burn something. A large proportion of our incendiary fires originate in this way. Others are instigated by strong drink to theft. *Kleptomania*, the insane desire to steal, is often awakened by alcohol. "I have known," says Prof. Monroe, "ladies of good position in society, who after a dinner or supper party, and after having taken sundry glasses of wine, could not resist the temptation of taking home any little article not their own; and who, in their sober moments, have returned them as if taken by mistake."

But the most common effect of alcohol is to prompt those who have taken it to deeds of violence. Very many, perhaps the majority of those who are addicted to the excessive use of ardent spirits, are excited by them to injure human beings, or to destroy human life. Men who, when sober, are not disposed to harm anybody, are roused by strong drink to a homicidal fury. The first person that crosses their path may be the victim of their rage, though it is more likely to be wreaked upon the helpless wife and babes at home.  Nine-tenths, perhaps a larger proportion, of the assaults and the homicides that take place in our land, are the effect of intoxicating liquor.  I do not mean to say simply that these offenders committed these offences *while* they were drunk: I mean that they committed these offences simply and solely *because* they were drunk. The laconic and often-repeated verdict of the reporter is, in most of these cases, literally true: "Rum did it."  Of course many crimes are committed with malice "aforethought," as the legal phrase is; but even in these cases strong drink is often made accessory before the fact.  For the doing of a deed of violence, like that of Wilkes Booth, a glass of fiery spirit is found to be a good preparation.

Such, working-men, are some of the facts concerning the effects of strong drink upon the body and the mind of the man that uses it.  The facts are not new, but I think that they are true.  At any rate, I have not meant to overstate any thing.  And it seems to me that I have given you some strong reasons for letting the vile stuff entirely alone.  It will do you no good unless you are sick; and if you are, you had better let the doctor be the judge whether you need it or not.  It costs some of you a good deal in the course of the year; times would be easier with you right away, if you would abstain from the use of it. It reduces the strength of your bodies, it weakens your power of endurance, it predisposes you to disease, it dulls your wits, and blunts your moral sense; it awakens and reinforces all that is coarsest and most devilish in your natures, and beats down every sentiment of purity and honor. Of all the enemies of the working-men, the worst is strong drink. If that were conquered and banished, the rest of their wrongs could be easily righted.

# VIII.

## THE DUTIES OF EMPLOYERS.

" MASTERS, give unto your servants that which is just and equal." So wrote a good man of the olden time to certain slaveholders whom he knew. If this was good counsel for the owners of slaves, it is certainly quite as good for the employers of free working-men. Freemen have at least as much right as bondmen to justice and equity. The abolition of slavery does not cancel the moral obligation of the man that organizes and directs labor, to deal fairly and mercifully with those in his employ.

Of this moral obligation, law and political economy take very little notice. Our laws are sometimes said to be founded on justice, but it is justice of a negative sort. They undertake to protect individuals in their rights; to defend them, that is, against wrongs; to prevent injustice, not to secure justice in any affirmative way: that is beyond the scope of human government. "The proper business of legislation," says Dr. Hopkins, "is to secure to all their rights, and not to oblige any to do right. If there are courts of equity, their object is not to compel the doing of right, but to prevent the doing of wrong through the imperfections and under the forms of law. That legislation should seek to pass from the guardianship of right to an attempt to compel the doing of right, is natural; but this has seldom been done without confusion and mischief."

In the matter of wages, the law leaves me free to dispose of my services for such a reward as suits me, and only stands by to guarantee the fulfilment of the contract thus freely made. My employer, taking advantage of my necessities, may agree to pay me less than a fair price for my work; but the law will not compel him to pay me any more than he agrees to pay me.

So with political economy. The fundamental principle in all its speculations is self-interest, not benevolence nor justice. It is assumed by the political economists, that men will always do what is for their interest; the idea is distinctly repudiated, that they will, as a rule, govern themselves by considerations of charity or of abstract morality. What are called the laws of political economy are therefore statements, not of what men ought to do, but of what experience shows that they will do. They are natural laws, — laws of a nature that is fallen from its normal condition, and only in part restored; laws to be studied, then, as one studies the law of gravitation or the law of chemical affinity, but by no means always·to be obeyed. The facts this science gives us are to be respected, as the facts that medical science gives us concerning epidemics are to be respected; but they are not to be acquiesced in as representing the best conceivable conditions of human society.

The New Testament morality gives us not merely the hard facts of human life, but the principles by which life in this world is to be regenerated, and made to conform to the divine ideal. Political economy tells us what the laws of exchange are: the New Testament shows what the relations of men ought to be. The one talks of market value and normal value, of the tendency of profits, and of supply and demand: the other speaks of justice and equity, of love and self-sacrifice. And the gospel encourages the hope, that, as the principles of Christ's teachings get more and more firmly fixed in the lives of men, these maxims of a higher morality will come to be recognized as setting forth the only true relations between man and man.

It is to these principles, then, as they affect the relations of employer and laborer, that I wish to call your attention now. We pray that Christ's kingdom may come: ought we not to know what it will bring with it when it comes? Ought we not to be preparing the way for its coming?

If "that which is just and equal" is to be the standard by which dealings between employers and workmen are to be measured, then it is plain that the employer and the workman are to deal with one another not as classes, but as individuals. Justice and equity, in the New Testament sense, are not collective or impersonal virtues: they are strictly personal. The class of employers and the class of laborers cannot adjust their relations on moral grounds, because it is not possible to hold a class of persons to moral responsibility. If masters are to give to their servants that which is just and equitable, then masters must put themselves into personal relations with their servants, and must treat them not as chattels, not as counters in the great game of commerce, not as stock or machinery, not as classes, but as persons, with a conscientious regard for their physical and moral welfare.

The tendency of modern industry is to separate the employer from the workman by a constantly widening interval. When all the work of the world was done by hand or with rude machinery, in small shops or factories, master and man were brought into close relations. The mill-owner or the master-mechanic not only knew the men in his employ, but often wrought by their side. Moreover, there was no such disparity of social conditions as we now see between employers and laborers. The princely fortunes, now so common, were then as rare; the capitalist was not, as a rule, raised very high above the social rank of the laborer. The effect of the improvement of machinery, and of the combination and subdivision of labor, has been twofold. On the one hand, vast numbers of laborers are now brought together by a single man, who deals with them largely through hired superintendents or overseers, and scarcely ever knows even the names of the people on his pay-roll. On the other hand, under this large system of manufactures, it is possible for men of organizing ability and energy to amass enormous wealth; so that they are separated socially, from the people they employ, by a distance almost as great as that which divides an English duke from the peasantry on his estates. Many of them, too, have their homes in cities far distant from their mills or their furnaces; and thus the opportunity for acquaintance with their employés is greatly diminished.

Not only so, but a large part of the production of

the country is now done by corporations; and most of the capitalists that organize and control the business have in this case nothing whatever to do with the work-people. The agent that manages the work for them sometimes has a limited interest in the profits of production; but he is usually a salaried man, and he understands that what is wanted of him is, to make the annual dividends on the stock as large as possible. The operatives know him only as the representative of the corporation: they hear him say that he is limited in his actions by the authority of the corporation; if he deals hardly with them, they are given to understand that it is by order of the board of directors, and that he has no alternative in the matter. Who or what this corporation is, they do not know at all. Perhaps they have never heard the names of the capitalists that constitute and control it. It is a great impersonal force, a mighty commercial machine; and to expect of it a just consideration, or a nice regard for the equities of contracts, would be of course preposterous. " Corporations have no souls:" how, then, can they govern themselves, in their relations with the persons in their employ, by high moral considerations?

This tendency to separate the capitalist and the laborer, either through the intervention of corporations, or through the building up of immense industrial concerns by individuals or firms, is one of the things to be deplored and resisted by all employers that mean to govern themselves by the Christian law. I do not condemn the large system of industry. It is doubtless better that much of the work of manufacturing should be done on a grand scale. Division of labor greatly reduces the cost of production; and the cheaper the products of industry can be made, the better it is for all classes. But it is not well, and it is not necessary, that the proprietor of a large establishment should withdraw himself from all personal relations with his work-people. It is quite possible for him to know them well, and to study how he may fulfil the injunction of the apostle, and give unto them that which is just and equal. He is in some degree responsible for their welfare, and he ought not to ignore them.

Neither is it necessary that the persons who constitute our great corporations should be wholly ignorant of the condition of the people in their employ. If the corporation has no soul, each individual member of it has one; and he is bound to think, not only of the dividends upon his stock, and how they may be enlarged, but also of the well-being of the men and women and children through whose labor his capital is utilized and increased. The bond of moral obligation that unites him to them is a strong one, and

he must not try to release hmself from it.   He ought
to insist, for one thing, that the agent to whom the
management of the business is intrusted shall be a
man not only of executive ability, but of large and
wise humanity, who will deal with working-people as
though they were human beings, and will study their
interests, as well as the interests of the stockholders.

I know that there are capitalists among us, members of corporations, who do think of these things,
and whose power is steadily exerted in behalf of
the working-people.   The men that own our mills
and our mines are not all greedy, hard-hearted, unscrupulous beings : very many of them are honestly
trying to temper the hard facts of business life with
Christian love.   Agents, too, there are, that are
always thoughtful of the welfare of the workmen ;
that would not hold their places for one hour unless
they were permitted to deal fairly and mercifully
with their hired laborers.  A very large proportion of
the employers of labor are men of this character; and
their humane regard for the people in their employ
is manifested sometimes in a very practical way.
For though the profits of business are sometimes
large, and the capitalist's gains are rapid then, at
other times, as at present, the losses are constant;
and but for the accumulations of more prosperous
seasons, the business must stop altogether, and the

laborers must suffer for the lack of employment. Long periods frequently occur in which the workmen are paid literally out of the pockets of the employers; in which, for the sake of keeping the mills running, and the work-people from want, the employers grow poorer instead of richer, month after month. Everybody knows that such cases occur, and they show that capitalists in New England do take thought for their laborers as well as themselves.

But, unfortunately, we are all familiar with instances of a different character, in which the greed of the capitalist has led to heartless and extortionate treatment of working-people. I knew of one corporation, in a distant city, that discharged a most competent and faithful agent, because he devoted a large part of his Sundays and of his evenings to the promotion of the welfare and happiness of the operatives under his care. The directors seemed to think that he was not sufficiently hard-fisted and stony-hearted for their purposes, and they turned him out. I am happy to learn that their business has never prospered since it left his hands.

Though such cases as these are, I hope, exceptional, yet they illustrate the point I am trying to make, — that the tendency of the large system of industry is to render capital impersonal, and thus unmoral, if not immoral, in its relations to labor.

It is a tendency that may be, and often is, successfully resisted; but it is only resisted by a resolute
determination on the part of individual capitalists to
rule their business by the Christian law. So long as
the wages system prevails (and it will not be superseded for many years), the employers of labor will
be, to some degree, responsible for the well-being
of the mechanics and operatives. The power that
wealth gives them, especially when it is centralized
and consolidated in great stock-companies, is a power
that carries with it heavy obligations. Let me mention, a little more specifically, a few of these.

First among them is the obligation of the capitalist
to care for the physical health and comfort of his
work-people. Some kinds of labor are almost necessarily injurious to health; but any kind of work
will kill if carried on in badly lighted and imperfectly ventilated rooms. The employer is bound to
make this a subject of study, and to have his rooms
so arranged and fitted up as to secure in them light
and warmth, and fresh wholesome air. Whatever aid
science can give him in the solution of this problem,
he ought to avail himself of. There are health-
saving as well as labor-saving contrivances in these
better days of ours; and the humane employer will,
if he is able, provide the one kind as promptly as the
other. He knows, or ought to know, more about

the conditions of health than his work-people do; and his knowledge, as fast as he acquires it, ought to be used for their benefit.

It is for his interest to do this. If the work-place is bright, airy, comfortable, and the workers feel well at their work, they will accomplish more, will do their work better, and will be much less likely to become discontented and disorderly. Money invested in improvements intended to add to the cheerfulness and healthfulness of the work is always well invested. But even if it were not, the obligation would rest with equal weight upon the employer. If he provides the place in which his work is done, he ought to provide a good place, and to see to it that those in his employ do not suffer any bodily damage that he can prevent.

It sometimes happens that workmen resent and hinder the efforts that are made for this object. Mr. Charles Reade gives us what I take to be well-accredited facts in his story, "Put Yourself in His Place," by which the perversity of workmen in this matter is illustrated. When a master-workman provided fans to remove the metal dust and stone grit arising from the grinding of saws, his hands refused to put them in gear, preferring to go on inhaling disease with every breath. Not until he had discharged several of them for neglecting to avail themselves of the health-saving apparatus provided for them, could he succeed in bringing it into use. But even if the laborers are indifferent or hostile to such measures, that is no reason for neglecting them. The opportunity and the power given to every employer ought to be beneficently used. Much has been done of late in this direction. In most work-places, the conditions are now more favorable to health than they formerly were. Ventilation is generally attempted, ceilings are higher, rooms are kept at a more uniform temperature, and in many ways work is rendered pleasanter and more healthful. Doubtless there is more that can be done, and good employers will not forget to do it.

Again: it appears to be the dictate at once of sound policy and of good principles, that employers should always treat their help with polite consideration. A true gentleman will remember that he is a gentleman, in his dealings with those in his employ, and will conduct himself so that they too will have no difficulty in finding it out. He will neither swear nor storm nor scold at them; he will not carry himself in their presence as though he thought them an inferior race of beings: he will bestow on them a civility exactly equal to that with which he treats the head of his commission-house in the city. If it is necessary for him to give an order, he will give it

in tones that suggest no arrogance; if it is necessary for him to administer a reproof, he will do it
without pitching his voice in the key of exaspera-
tion. It may be perfectly understood among his
work-people, that his orders are on no account to be
disobeyed, and yet his whole bearing toward them
may be that of the most perfect courtesy.

One of the truest gentlemen I ever knew was the
superintendent of a large gang of navvies. His
treatment of them was always affable and kind: he
never raised his voice, or roughened his tones, in
addressing them; he had a way of being obeyed,
but he made no noise about it; and the consequence
was, that he never had the slightest trouble from
insubordination, and his men came to have unbounded regard for him.

The dictatorial, domineering ways of some employers are exceedingly exasperating to working-
people. They feel that they are wronged by such
treatment, and they are. Every man, poor or rich,
hod-carrier or capitalist, has a right to respectful
treatment. "Be courteous" is the gospel rule of
good manners, and the injunction is not limited. The
people whom you employ are not excepted. Your
obligation to treat them politely is just as binding as
your obligation to deal with them honestly.

This rule ought to be understood as applying to

the kitchens, as well as to the shops and the mills.
The duty of the parlor to treat the kitchen courte-
ously is not often recognized. Indeed, I should not
wonder if the bare suggestion would provoke the mer-
riment of some who read these words. But, ladies,
it is an obligation that cannot be set aside. Your
servant-girls have just as good a right to be politely
treated by you as your afternoon callers have. True
Christian courtesy is not reserved for people who
wear fine raiment: it falls like the dew, without par-
tiality, on weed and flower. You may be as positive
in the laws of your household, and as thorough in
their enforcement, as you please; but there is no need
of scolding. A servant that you cannot control by
gentle measures, you cannot control at all. And it
is entirely possible, without abrogating the authority
that belongs to you as mistress of the house, and
without taking your domestics into your confidence,
to treat them always with a gentle and gracious consideration which shall be as grateful to them as it is
honorable to you.

For the intellectual improvement of their working-
people, employers ought to have a care. Wherever
large numbers of operatives are gathered, they ought
to be encouraged and assisted in forming lyceums,
and collecting libraries. In all such efforts to
improve themselves, laborers should feel that they

have the hearty co-operation of capitalists. In Lonsdale, R. I., I found, on a recent visit, a large and beautiful building erected by the proprietors of the mill, and devoted almost wholly to the instruction and diversion of the working-people. It contained a well-selected library, rooms for debating-clubs and social meetings, and a fine hall, capable of seating more than a thousand people, in which every winter a course of entertainments, consisting of literary and scientific lectures, with a few more popular amuse-ments, is given at very low cost to the operatives and their families. The hall is free; and a thousand season - tickets, at a dollar each, easily pays for procuring ten or a dozen good entertainments. It was pleasant to see the effect of this provision upon the characters of the work-people. I found in that hall the largest and one of the most intelligent lecture - audiences that I ever addressed in New England; and the next day in the great mill, and throughout the village, the signs of refinement and contentment were everywhere visible. It was good to know that one of the most powerful manufactur-ing companies in New England was using its power in a manner so beneficent.

I shall not be disputed, either, if I affirm that employers ought to be interested in the moral and religious welfare of the persons in their employ. It

is true that the relation of employer and laborer is a
business relation; and it may be said, that if the
employer goes outside of the contract, and interests
himself in the moral and religious condition of his
work-people, he is meddling with what is none of
his business. Doubtless he may do this officiously
and offensively; but it is possible also, I think, that,
without appearing in any way to overstep the proprieties of the relation, he may take a deep interest
in the higher welfare of the people who work for
him. The Christian law is, that we are to do good
to all men as we have opportunity; and certainly
the employer's opportunity is among his employés.
If his treatment of them is what I have suggested
it should be, and if in his business relations with
them he is always prompt and upright, he will
certainly have their respect, and, if he chooses, may
exert a strong influence over them. Without
seeming in any way to dictate with regard to their
conduct, he may, by a kind word spoken now and
then, by advice not too obtrusively offered, by an
expression of solicitude, by a hearty approval of
efforts to do right, confer upon them incalculable
benefits. It seems to me that every employer ought
to regard the people in his employ as his parish;
that he ought to be always on the alert to find
opportunities and ways of doing them good. If any

of them are addicted to vice, he will know it; and he ought to study how he may reclaim them. If any of them are sick or in want, he may, by a little attention and sympathy, not only minister to their comfort, but also increase his power over them for their good. Among those in his employ there may be young people away from home : in their welfare he ought to take a special interest. His relation to them should be as nearly as possible a paternal relation : as far as he is able, he should supply to them the restraint and the counsel with which they parted when they left their homes. There are those, it is true, who do not care for such counsel; and upon them it would be unwise to press kind offices that they do not appreciate. But there are many others of a different spirit; and without any formal proffer of friendship the employer may easily enough convey to the young men and women at work for him the impression that he is willing to act the part of a friend, if they need one. Such a personal interest in them, made manifest in some respectful and unobtrusive way, would be of great service to many of them.

When persons come from abroad into your employ, it may not be amiss for you to inquire of them what church they have been in the habit of attending, and to put them in communication with some pastor of that denomination in your town. If it turns out that they have not been in the habit of going to church, you might properly enough mention to them the names of those churches in which you know that they would be welcome. One or two employers hire seats in my church for their employés. I am so old-fashioned as to believe that going to church is a good habit, and that people addicted to it are, as a general rule, steadier, more industrious, and more virtuous, than those who are not.

I have been writing on the supposition that you are living for some higher object than simply to make money. If that is your chief end, I am aware that these suggestions will seem to you very impracticable. Doubtless it is not well, if that is all that a man is after, that he should have much care for other people's interests.

A keen article about our millionaires, in a recent magazine, closed by giving some of the indispensable conditions of attaining to millionism; and these are three of them : —

"You must devote your life to the getting and keeping of other men's earnings."

"You must care little or nothing about other men's wants or sufferings or disappointments."

"You must not mind it, that great wealth involves many others' poverty."

I can easily see that this may be true. And therefore, if any of you care more to be millionaires than for any thing else in the world, I am sure you will pay no heed whatever to that I have said. You can't afford to get your sympathies involved in the welfare of the people you employ, if this is your object in life. You had better keep at a distance from them, deal with them wholly through subordinates, shut your ears and your hearts to their needs and their troubles.

But I should be sorry to believe that any of the employers that read this are living for such an object. I have no doubt that it is the honest purpose of all of them, to do some good in the world as they go along; and, this being their purpose, I cannot think of any field of usefulness nearer or more promising than that which is open to them among the persons in their employ.

I believe heartily in colleges, and missionary societies, and Bible societies, and all such enterprises of benevolence, and want to do what I can to help them; but if the impossible should come to pass, and some rich relative should die, and leave me a million of dollars, I am not at all certain that I should distribute it among the benevolent societies, or use it in founding a college. If I had a sufficient knowledge of business to warrant me in organizing some productive industry by which a large number of persons might find employment and livelihood, by which a number of families might be gathered into a community, and aided by such counsel and oversight as I could give in living comfortably and healthily and intelligently and purely, I do not know but I should think that a better thing to do than to found a college, or endow a publication society. To use such a business relation as that benevolently ; to help some of my poorer neighbors in helping themselves, to find my pleasure and my reward in making the way of life a little plainer and a little smoother and a little brighter for them ; to make them sharers with me in the joint rewards of their labor and my capital, and to aid them in getting on their own feet and standing in their lot in some manly and independent fashion, — such a work as this, if I only knew enough to do it, would give me greater satisfaction than any thing else I could do; and I doubt whether any way of using money could be devised more truly benevolent or Christian than this.

Are not such opportunities on a larger or a smaller scale open to all of you, gentlemen capitalists ? and is there any better way for you to serve Christ and your country than to put yourselves thus into kindly and helpful relations with the people you employ ?

Many of those who have amassed wealth find

their pleasure in improving the soil, or the domestic animals: perhaps the time may come when the improvement of the condition and the character of human beings will afford to some good men an equal pleasure. It is not by alms or largesses that we wisely aid our fellow-men, but by encouraging them in their efforts to take care of themselves. There is a great field here for philanthropic labor; and the time will come, I doubt not, when good men will be ready to occupy it.

# IX.

## THE FUTURE OF LABOR.

"THE country clergyman is the poor man's only friend," wrote an English rector's wife to John Ruskin. "Alas, I know it," was the reply, "and too well. What can be said of more deadly and ghastly blame against the clergy of England, or any other country, than that they are the poor man's only friends? Have they, then, so betrayed their Master's charge and mind in their preaching to the rich, so smoothed their words and so sold their authority, that, after twelve hundred years intrusting of the gospel to them, there is no man in England who will have mercy on the poor but they?"

To this condemnation, ministers of the gospel, even here in New England, are continually exposed. There is imminent danger that our churches, instead

of shaping society, will be shaped by society; that
the laws of nature, working themselves out in the
world of finance and exchanges, will domineer the
Christian law; that the fissure now running through
the social world, and threatening to become a great
gulf fixed between the employing and the laboring
classes, will divide the religious world as well: so
that there shall be a system of caste recognized and
established in our churches; so that the rich shall
meet by themselves in the grand churches, and the
poor in the mission-chapels; and there shall be no
sympathy nor communion between the two classes,
but only alms, with a certain haughty condescension
on the one side, and a qualified mendicancy, with
envious resentment, on the other. This is the danger,
I say, to which our Christianity is exposed here in
New England, and especially in our manufacturing
cities and villages. It is nothing occult, mystical,
visible only to the eye of the seer: it is right before
our faces; the wayfaring man, though ever so heed-
less, cannot help seeing it. And when you speak
of it to faithful and self-denying ministers and lay-
men, the common answer is confession. " I know it:
it is a great pity; but what can you do about it?
You must take society as it is, and make your work
conform to its usages. There is no use in running a
muck against the social tendencies of the day." All

the while the breach grows wider. There is no lack of organized charities, hospitals, homes, relief agencies, city missions, and all that; but I sometimes think these very agencies aggravate the evil. A man wants sympathy, and we give him a soup-ticket; he needs friendly counsel, and we commend him to the soft side of a charitable board. Thus our very charity becomes impersonal and indiscriminate, serves only to separate still more widely those whom Christ died to bring together. Of

> " Almsgiving through a door that is
> Not open enough for two friends to kiss,"

there is plenty : of the Christian practice of bearing one another's burdens there is less and less as our civilization increases in complexity. This fact is what adds such pungency to that terrible satire, published a few months ago, entitled, "Modern Christianity a Civilized Heathenism." This is the sad result to which Mr. Ruskin points in the words of upbraiding which I quoted above. Quite willing, far too willing, are most of our good Christians to let the clergyman be the poor man's only friend; to turn over to him the duty of caring for the lowlier classes of society; to make him a sort of charitable middle-man whose function it is to keep the poor from troubling the rich, and the rich from taking thought for the poor.

For my own part, I quite decline to stand in any such position as this. It is the business of the people, as well as of the minister, to know the poor that are always with us, and to study the hard problems of their present and their future. It is the minister's duty to protest, in the name of Jesus of Nazareth, against the division of the Church and of society into jealous and unsympathizing classes. It is the duty of the minister to tell the poor and the ignorant that they are often wickedly envious and suspicious of the rich; that they incase themselves, not seldom, in such an armor of distrustfulness and surliness that nobody can get near them in any friendly way; that the prosperity of their neighbors, at which they are often angry, is not always owing to the fact that their neighbors are more dishonest or more unscrupulous than they are, but often to the fact that their neighbors are more industrious and more prudent than they are. It is my duty thus to warn the poor against bitterness and injustice in their judgments of the rich. I have been poor myself, and know, by the teachings of my own heart, just how wickedly poor people often feel toward those who are better off for this world.

On the other hand, it is the minister's duty to warn

the rich against the indifference and contempt with which they often treat their poorer neighbors, and to admonish them that the gospel of Christ requires of those who possess wealth or culture or power a benevolent use of it, as good stewards of God's manifold grace; to declare to them, in season and out of season, that part of the counsel of God which makes it plain that the careless or selfish handling of property or knowledge will bring a curse to its possessor; and to bid them, again and again, " to look not every man on his own things, but also on the things of others."

Moreover, it is the preacher's duty to show to both classes, and to all classes in society, that they are bound together in a community of interests, so that one class cannot suffer without bringing suffering upon all the rest; so that no class can rise to any sure eminence, or any permanent power, by the degradation of the rest.

I do not believe that the descendants of the Pilgrim Fathers are unwilling to recognize the practical bearings of Christian principles. Therefore I ask you now to study for a little while the question of the working-man's future, — a question in which, if our religion is true, the manufacturer and the merchant and the professional man are interested not much less deeply than the working-man himself. I ask you to consider it, not as capitalists, nor as traders, nor as politicians, nor as the disciples of economic schools, nor as trades-unionists, nor as Sovereigns of Industry; but as citizens, as philanthropists, as disciples of Jesus Christ. What is to become of the working-man?

1. Of those who would remand him to the bondage from which, after centuries of degradation, he has escaped, and make him the chattel of his employer, there are almost none among us; so that we may dismiss that contingency, as among things so unlikely as to be morally impossible.

2. In certain states of society different from ours, we should expect to find a considerable number of those who, like Mr. Ruskin, would be glad to see a modified type of feudalism restored. In his "Fors Clavigera," this eminent author urges, with all that passionate eloquence of which he is a master, the re-establishment of this relation between the employer and the employed; so that on the one hand there shall be a gentle and gracious guardianship, and on the other a loving dependence; so that the two races of masters and of servants, of which we read in the Waverley Novels, shall again return to earth. The spirit in which Mr. Ruskin writes is of the highest; and his demand for a nearer personal relation between the two classes is the one to which, following him a long way off, I have tried to give

expression. The fact that he has devoted a large portion of his wealth to the purchase of a tract of land upon which he proposes to carry out his theory by employing men and women to work for him, in whose welfare and that of their children he will take a kindly care, convinces the average British economist that he has gone mad. Well, be it so: that was what they said about Christ when he began to unfold his simple laws of ministry and sacrifice. Only I cannot help wishing that some tens of thousands more of the rich and cultivated people of both continents might be bitten with the same madness that now afflicts John Ruskin.

Still, though the spirit in which he writes and works is the very spirit of the Nazarene; and though, while the present system of industry continues, no better result can be hoped for than that the hearts of the masters should be turned to the servants, and the hearts of the servants to the masters, — nothing is plainer than that Mr. Ruskin's Utopia will not stand, in the latter day, upon the earth. While the wealth of the world belongs, as now, to the few, it is of course devoutly to be desired, that, between the opulent few and the dependent many, there should be a relation of gracious care on the one side, and of thankful loyalty on the other. Such a relation is infinitely better than the present conflict

13

of haughty greed with resentful suspicion; but be the dependence of ever so happy and contented a type, we hope there is something far better in store for the many; and, in our present inquiry, we are looking to see what that shall be.

3. The policy of the trades-unions is exactly the opposite of that urged by Mr. Ruskin; namely, the arraying of the laboring-classes in a warfare against their employers. By such an organized conflict with the class of capitalists, the trades-unionists seem to suppose that they may permanently improve the condition of the laboring class; that they may conquer in war some advantages that would not accrue to them under the reign of peaceful industry and free competition.

Three principal methods are resorted to by the unions. First, they demand increased wages, and refuse to work if the demand is not conceded. Second, they endeavor to prevent an increase in the number of laborers. Third, they try to enforce rules for increasing the amount of work. As to the first of these methods, I have said already that it is perfectly lawful, provided that violence is let alone, and no attempt is made to force unwilling workmen to join the strike. It may often be foolish, and morally unjustifiable, to demand higher wages, because it may be that the wages refused are as

large as can be paid without ruining the business :
but freedom to work involves the freedom to refrain
from working ; and it would be neither politic nor
just to deny to workmen the right of combining to
secure their own interests.

As to the other methods, which attempt the
reduction of the number of laborers by forbidding
apprentices, and preventing non-union men from
working, and which seek to increase the number of
day's-works to be done, by making rules that men
shall work slowly, and do their work poorly, so that
it shall quickly wear out and need to be replaced,
they are at once barbarous and absurd. "You are
strictly cautioned," says a by-law of the Bradford
(England) Bricklayers' Laborers, "not to overstep
good rules by doing double work, and causing
others to do the same, in order to gain a smile from
the master. Such foolhardy and deceitful actions
leave a great portion of good members out of
employment. Certain individuals have been guilty,
who will be expelled if they do not refrain." . . .
The Manchester Bricklayers' Association have a rule
providing that "any man found running or working
beyond a regular speed shall be fined 2*s*. 6*d*. for the
first offence, 5*s*. for the second, 10*s*. for the third,
and, if still persisting, shall be dealt with as the
committee think proper. . . . During the building

of the Manchester Law Courts, the bricklayers' laborers struck, because they were desired to wheel bricks, instead of carrying them on their shoulders." [1]

By such regulations as these, everywhere enforced, the trades-unions seem to suppose that they can improve the condition of their members.

But such regulations, intended as they are to hinder and cripple production, to keep men out of work who need to work, and to restrict the gains of labor to a small class, are not only contrary to all true economy, but to every just principle of human rights and human progress. It is for the interest of the whole world, that every man in it shall have a chance to work when he wants to work, and shall be encouraged to do good work; in no other way can the aggregate wealth of the world be increased; and the larger the aggregate wealth of the world, the larger, if exchanges are unrestricted, will each man's portion be. All methods that are intended to diminish the total result of human industry are essentially vicious; and it would seem as if even a dullard might see that they must be. Moreover, these regulations to which I have referred are meant to secure the aggrandizement of one class by the injury of other classes. You will never prosper in that way, my friends. You cannot rise by tram-

---

[1] Thornton on Labor, quoted by Prof. Cairnes.

pling your neighbors under your feet. No man's rights can be established by doing wrong to his fellow-man.

Mr. Thornton, a distinguished advocate of the Labor Leagues in England, bears this testimony: "Whether a country be stationary or progressive, an exceptionally high rate of wages cannot be maintained in any particular trade, unless the workmen of all other trades are prevented from entering that particular trade, and endeavoring to get the same rate. Unionism cannot keep up the rate in one trade without keeping it down in others."[1]

That is just as plain as the daylight; and therefore one is quite justified in saying with Prof. Cairnes that trades-unionism, so far as it operates by these restrictive rules of labor, "is, in its essential character, a monopoly of the narrowest kind; capable, indeed, of accomplishing some small results in favor of a privileged few, but wholly destitute of efficacy as an expedient for helping social improvement; a monopoly, moreover, founded on no principle either

[1] Mr. Thornton undertakes to show that this method, though its advantages are secured to but few workmen *at a time* and to these at the expense of the rest, may be gradually extended, until its benefits shall be shared by the whole laboring-class; but, as Prof. Cairnes clearly points out, the efficacy of the plan depends wholly on the fact that it creates a monopoly; and "the extension of its privileges to the whole population would be equivalent to their entire abrogation." See his Political Economy, p. 246, *et seq.*

of moral desert or of industrial efficiency, but simply on chance or arbitrary selection; which, therefore, cannot but exert a demoralizing influence on all who come within its scope; in all its aspects presenting an ungracious contrast to all that is best and most generous in the spirit of modern democracy." It is not by such methods that the future welfare of the working-man will be promoted. Every resort to these exclusive and despotic practices postpones the day of his full enfranchisement.

4. It would seem as if some sense of the inefficacy, if not of the immorality, of these methods, is beginning to dawn upon the men that have been at the head of the trades-unions in this country; for I notice that some of them are beginning openly to discuss another project, namely, the forcible seizure of the mills and the factories. Either this, or a political revolution placing in power a government that shall proceed to take possession of the property of the country, and administer it for the equal benefit of all individuals, would seem to be the present ambition of some of these astute philosophers. Between these two methods, I do not know that there is much to choose. If the policy of pillage is to prevail, we may as well be pillaged by a mob armed with bludgeons, as by another mob armed with the forms of law. For of these schemes, as of all social-

istic schemes that involve the abolition of private property, and the re-distribution of wealth according to some *à priori* theory of justice, the essence is simply pillage. The fundamental maxim of the radical socialists is, that property is robbery; and fortified by this maxim, they propose to take by force the wealth of the world from those who now possess it, and who have no right to it, as they say, and give it to somebody else, who certainly has no better right to it. This is a queer method of restitution. This whole socialistic movement is philosophically absurd. The doctrine that property is robbery, is a good doctrine for robbers, and also for paupers, but not for men to whom manhood means something more than subsistence. Mr. Herbert Spencer has an answer to this doctrine, which can hardly be improved: —

"If all property is robbery, then, among other consequences, it follows that a man can have no right to the things he consumes for food. And if these are not his before eating them, how can they become his at all? As Locke asks, When do they begin to be his? when he digests, or when he eats, or when he boils, or when he brings them home? If no previous act can make them his property, neither can the power of assimilation do it, nor even their absorption into the tissues. Wherefore, pursuing the idea, we arrive at the conclusion, that as the whole of his bones, muscles, skin, &c., have been built up from nutriment not belonging to him, a man has no property in his own flesh and blood, can have no valid title to himself, has no more claim to his own limbs than he has to the limbs of another, and has as good a right to his neighbor's body as to his own."

That is the fundamental principle of socialism, reduced to its lowest terms. A neater example of *reductio ad absurdum* it would be hard to find.

This proposition to abolish private property, and establish the commune instead, is not at all likely to find favor among American working-men. They have sense enough to know that such a system must rest its foundations on organized rapine, and that, even if it could once be founded, the practical difficulties in the way of the distribution of wealth by means of it would be insuperable.[1] But apart from these enormities, they know full well that the commune is not the school in which to train *men*. Any organization that takes away from individuals the opportunity and the need of self-reliance is fatal to all high character. We have seen the communistic principle at work among us on a small scale, and what have been the results? Look at such communities as the Shakers, the Mormons, the Oneida Community. What chance is there in them for a man

[1] See Appendix A.

to develop his own individuality? What opportunity for the cultivation of self-reliance?

It is claimed by the advocates of these systems,
that the competitions of society are too fierce, that
they breed disorders, that they sour and spoil the
characters of men; and they base an argument for
their societies upon the fact that they exclude these
competitions. Doubtless it is true that the contests
in which men must take part, if they would make
their way through life, are often heated and severe;
doubtless there is need that the principle of good-
will should come in to temper their severities: yet
there can be no manhood that is not wrought out
through conflict. Take a child that has been coddled
and petted at home, that has had no experience of
the buffetings of the play-ground or the street: what
does he amount to? Yet it is just such characters
as these that the socialistic communities must inevitably produce, if they are what they pretend to be.
In these societies, no man depends upon himself for
maintenance: he depends upon the community. He
does not choose his own courses of life: they are
chosen for him by the community. He does not
forge for himself the weapons with which to wage
the warfare of life: they are furnished him out of
the armory of the community. Consequently there
can be no such thing as high and strong individual

character in such a society. That can only be developed by standing alone, and working out the questions of existence in manly independence. In such a society, where people dress alike, work alike, live alike in all particulars, they finally come to look alike and to think alike and to talk alike. The uniformity becomes hateful and distressing to see. It is utter stagnation. The soul loses sight of the grand possibilities of life; it sinks down upon the dead level of conventions, and the man becomes only a part of a great social machine.

Is not this true? You have long been hearing of these societies and their doings: have you heard of their developing any high grade of character? The Shakers make excellent hats and brooms; they sell us the best of garden seeds and healing herbs; they raise very large beets and squashes; they produce a very fair article of apple-sauce. But what sort of *men* do they produce? Do *they* amount to any thing? The same question may be asked, with the same result, in regard to all the other communistic societies. The great body of the members are all on one level, and that a very low level, of attainment and character. I do not speak of their moral qualities, but of their mental proportions. The theory of these communities is, that all the members are equal in rank and influence; the fact is, I suspect, that one individual in each of them is the practical dictator, and the rest are only his subjects. There is but one man in Mormondom, and that is Brigham Young; there is but one man in the Oneida Community, — Mr. John Humphrey Noyes; Shakerdom has but one prophet, and his name is Frederick Evans. Each of these is a man of considerable force; but these are the whole product of their respective communities. The rest are nobodies.

This is the only true test of a social system, — tell us what kind of men it produces. It may be able to show better agriculture, more successful manufactures, a more economical adaptation of the physical forces, a better provision of creature comforts; but if, with all this, the men and women are a small-souled, dull-witted, inferior type of humanity, the system is a bad one. I do not think I am slandering anybody when I say that, tried by this test, these social communities are failures.

I would not have you think that this is the only or the worst evil connected with these societies, — that they destroy self-reliance, and thus depreciate individuality. Their repudiation of the family is a much greater offence. But the result to which I have pointed is enough to seal the condemnation of all communistic systems, and to show that it is not by any such methods that the working-men of the future will gain the greatest good of life.

If, then, it is not through bondage, nor through feudalism, nor through trades-unionism, nor through Communism, that the problem of the working-man's welfare is to find its solution, by what process shall he work it out? Is the present system of industry, with such mitigations of its hardships as Christian principle may be trusted to secure, the final answer to this question? If it is, then I fear we must say that the working-man's future is not very bright.

I have said, in my first chapter, that the effect of the introduction of machinery has been to raise, rather than to depress, the *real* wages of labor; to increase, that is, the amount of the necessaries of life a day's wages will buy. That statement has been confirmed by careful study. Still the improvement has been very slow, and there is no promise that it will be more rapid in the future. Those who earn their living by labor are a little better off, positively, than they were twenty-five or fifty years ago: relatively, they are not so well off as they were then. There has been an enormous increase of wealth; but the *proportion* of that wealth that has fallen to the laboring-classes is very small, and it is constantly growing smaller. And I believe that most of the

political economists are agreed in saying that this
state of things is sure to continue, under the present
system; that the tendency is toward an increasing
inequality of conditions; that, while the rich are
likely to grow richer, the poor will grow relatively
if not positively poorer. There is, as Prof. Cairnes
tells us, "a constant growth of the national capital,
accompanied with a nearly equally constant decline
in the *proportion* of capital which goes to support
productive labor." And this, as he says, can only
issue in one result; namely, " a harsh separation of
classes, combined with those glaring inequalities in
the distribution of wealth which most people will
agree are among the chief elements of our social
instability."

That is what the economists prophesy; and the
statistics, so far as I have been able to collate them,
confirm the prophecy. The prospect is not a
pleasant one to contemplate. It is not much comfort
to be told by an eminent professor that "a few, more
energetic or more fortunate than the rest, will from
time to time escape, as they do now, from the ranks
of their fellows to the higher walks of industrial life,"
when we are at the same time assured that "the
great majority will remain substantially where they
are," and that " the remuneration of labor, skilled or
unskilled, can never rise much above its present level."

There is one way out of this condition of helpless dependence; and that is by an organization of industry which shall encourage and assist the laborer in passing over to the ranks of the capitalists. [It is not by the abolition, but by the preservation in all its sacredness, of private property, and by bringing to bear upon the laborer all the motives to prudence, self-restraint, economy, and industry, that now actuate the capitalist in his accumulation of private property, that his condition will be improved. ]

It is not your interest nor mine, that the class of mere wage-laborers should remain as large as it is. We want to see it growing smaller year by year ; to see large numbers forsaking its ranks for the ranks of the capitalists ; rising up from a condition of absolute dependence to one of comparative independence. If we are philanthropists, if we are patriots, nay, if we are good and humane citizens, we are deeply interested in every movement that tends to give an increasing number of the people a proprietary interest in the wealth of the country. The centralization of capital is just what we do not want : [its widest possible diffusion is what we all desire, if we are wise. ]

We have always been saying that it is vastly better for the country that the land should belong to a large number of small farmers than that it should be in the hands of a few great proprietors, leaving the great body of the agriculturists to be either leaseholders or laborers. Why does not the same principle hold good in our mechanical industries? Why is it not to be desired, for the same reason, that as many as possible of the people that live by them should have a proprietary interest in them? Every man that owns a share in the business at which he works is by that fact made a better workman and a better citizen.

To be sure, the only way in which working-men can procure capital is to deny themselves, and save it. Sometimes they dream of getting it from the government; of having a great loan-agency established by law to provide laborers with the means for engaging in business either singly or in co-operative companies. But this is a wild notion. How can the government get the money? Only by taking it away from other citizens. Working-men cannot reasonably look for such subvention in their enterprises. They must stand on their own feet, and work out their own fortunes. If they can save their earnings, and combine them as capital, and thus become directly interested in the profits of their labor, they will in due time rise into a position of independence. This is what I believe they will learn to do in the future.

I have expressed this opinion pretty confidently in my second chapter; and the conclusion to which my own thinking has led me is one that the writers in Great Britain who have been brought to close quarters with this problem are almost unanimous in affirming. What John Stuart Mill has written, and what Thomas Hughes has said about it, I know; but these men might be suspected of a little sentimental aberration, and therefore I might not have dared to strengthen myself by their utterances. But when I find a Tory peer like Lord Derby declaring that the experiment of co-operation promises well, and ought to be fairly tried, and arguing that the principle is not discredited by the failures hitherto encountered in its practical working, inasmuch as almost every other great principle has been brought into operation through just such repeated failures; when I hear a rich contractor and employer of labor, like Mr. Thomas Brassey, saying, "We earnestly wish success to the experiment of adapting the co-operative principle to productive industry;" and when I find Prof. Cairnes of London (in whose decease, recently, all the leading English journals lament the loss of the ablest living political economist) writing that "Co-operation constitutes the one and only solution of our present problem, the sole path by which the laboring-classes as a whole, or even in any large number, can emerge from their condition of hand-to-mouth living, to share in the gains and honors of advancing civilization," — I think I may endure, with considerable equanimity, to hear it said (as in some quarters doubtless I shall) that the views I have here expressed show just how much a minister knows about business.[1]

And now my last word is, that every honest and well-considered effort on the part of working-men to put this principle into practice ought to have the encouragement of every one of us. We must not look upon these experiments from the standpoint of self-interest merely; we must not think to measure them with our yardsticks and our half-bushels; we must not weigh them solely with our steelyards: we must think of them as affecting the condition, and especially the character, of our neighbors; and if they are likely to result in good to human beings, then we ought to rejoice in them. We cannot afford to be angry with any thing that opens an ampler life, and supplies a higher motive, to any of our fellow-men.

It is only gradually, and by very slow degrees, that this principle of co-operation will be brought into use. But few of our working-men possess the requisite intelligence and self-control to qualify them

[1] See Appendix B.

14

for united action in this field. Here and there, in a small way, with many accompanying failures, the experiment will succeed. It is not going to revolutionize our trade or our industry in a year, or in ten years; but learning wisdom by defeat, and rising, as a class, steadily in the scale of intelligence, group after group of our best workmen may be expected to lift themselves out of dependence into a position in which they shall own the tools and the machinery and the stock with which they work, and enjoy the profits of the capital invested, as well as the wages of the work done. And every time that this is accomplished, every time that any company of workmen prove themselves capable of the foresight and the self-denial necessary to success in such a venture, all who love their fellow-men will thank God, and take courage; for every such success but opens and clears the path over which the millions in dependence and penury must pass into the competence and the peace of the better days to come.

# APPENDIX.

# A.

THE question of the feasibility of socialism is beginning
to be argued in certain quarters; and it is not unlikely to
be pushed into considerable prominence during the next
ten years. "The nationalization of capital" is what is
demanded by the advocates of this system; and by capital
they mean (I quote from one of them) "the machinery
of locomotion, the machinery of communication, the machinery of production, the machinery of distribution, and
the products of industry during the process of distribution." Whether legs are to be considered as part of the
"machinery of locomotion," and tongues as part of "the
machinery of communication," and whether these with
the railroads and the telegraph are to be "nationalized,"
our advocate does not tell us. It would seem, however,
to a casual visitor at Washington, that a sufficient number
of these unruly members are already "nationalized," and
that a project for the domestication of a few of them
should find favor with the working-classes. Indeed, the
vice of depending on the nation, instead of depending on

themselves, is one to which far too many of our citizens have been addicted ; and the proposition to make it the corner-stone of the social fabric should be carefully considered before it is adopted. The occupation of hanging upon the skirts of the government has not, as a general rule, proved a very efficient method of developing high character. Place-hunters are not, as a class, conspicuous for virtue or for usefulness. And it may well be questioned whether the plan of employing the whole population in pursuits of this nature would be found to promote either prosperity or morality.

The process of " nationalization," to which the advocate above quoted points us, is tolerably comprehensive. When " the machinery of locomotion, the machinery of communication, the machinery of production, the machinery of distribution, and the products of industry during the process of distribution," shall have been " nationalized," very little will be left for the individual. In what respect this project falls short of " the abolition of private property," with which our advocate professes to " have no sympathy," it would be hard to say. Possibly, under this scheme, a man might be permitted to own the house in which he lived ; but his farm, his garden, his tools, his stock in trade, must all be " nationalized," for they are all included in one or another of the categories mentioned. The letting of a house in which he did not live would not be allowed to him : all houses not occupied by their owners would become the property of the nation. Of course, no man would be permitted to receive any interest on the money that he had saved. Money saved

is capital in its simplest form, and all capital must be
" nationalized." There is a theory that rent is robbery,
and interest iniquity, and that no man ought to be
permitted to reap any benefit whatever from his own
prudence and self-denial. This theory is getting a hearing
among the working-men of this country, through various
pamphlets and other publications ; and it would seem that
the writer from whom I have quoted must have adopted
it for substance. It is only fair to him to quote at length
from a courteous letter addressed by him to one of the
daily journals, in answer to the positions taken in the last
chapter of this volume : —

" The new socialism claims that the great inventions of
the present century, which have multiplied so many
times man's power of production and locomotion, have
made it necessary for the most economical production and
distribution that large amounts of accumulated wealth —
or capital — should be employed in the methods of industry ; thus putting it in the power of those possessing
such wealth to obtain the ownership and control of more
and more of the national industry. That the aggregation
of wealth and power into the hands of fewer and fewer
of the people increases like a sum in compound interest.
That it makes the actual producers of the national wealth
more and more dependent upon the managers of their
industry. That it has formed a privileged class, rising to
be more powerful than the most powerful aristocracy the
world has ever been cursed with. That even in England,
that stronghold of aristocracy, lords and dukes have to

succumb to the merchants and manufacturers, and their grand ancestral estates are changing hands.

"They, the nobles themselves, are, in order to retain their political and social influence, submitting themselves to what, a few years ago, they considered the *degradation* of trade.

"In short, that steam has revolutionized the industry of the civilized world.

"How could we expect that any machinery of government could adapt itself without changes, almost, if not quite, revolutionary in character, to the new order of things?

"The new socialism demands that the changes in government made necessary by the progress of industry shall be put into operation with the least possible delay. . . . *If* ours is 'a government of the people, *by* the people and *for* the people,' and *if* the most important function of government is the protection of its individual citizens, they have a right to ask that this enormous power of owning and controlling the capital of the nation, which is the accumulated labor of the nation, and which directs and controls the industry of the nation, should be in the hands of the nation in its collective capacity, and not in the hands of private individuals and corporations to be used for their own profit and gain."

Why this should be called "the *new* socialism," I do not know. It does not appear to differ in any material respect from the socialism of Louis Blanc. All the theories here promulgated are urged with great vigor in

" The Organization of Labor ; " and they were put into partial operation in the French Revolution of 1848. They did not work very well in Paris at that day ; and we may be permitted to doubt whether they would be found any more practicable in Boston at this day.

Two important difficulties are encountered upon the threshold of this project. How, to begin with, would the government get possession of the capital of the nation ? " The new socialism " demands that the " revolutionary " changes in government, " made necessary by the progress in industry, shall be put into operation with the least possible delay." Exactly ; but how ? Not to speak of the railroads and the telegraph-lines, how is the nation to get possession of my rented house, of my neighbor's paper-mill, of the bank-stock and the mortgage-deeds upon the proceeds of which another neighbor — a widow with several children — is subsisting ? The expectation that individual owners will voluntarily give up to the government the property they have saved or inherited, will scarcely be entertained. This property must be taken from them by force ; and it will not be yielded up without a bloody struggle. Very few of those who have private possessions of any value will be in favor of these "revolutionary changes." Are the destitute classes of this country numerous enough and strong enough to take the property of the country, by force, from those who now hold it ? That is the practical question which confronts the advocates of " the new socialism." Before entering upon the civil war to which their theories instantly con-duct them, it would be well for them to count the cost.

But admitting that all the capital in the land could be
acquired by "the nation in its collective capacity," the
difficulties in the way of managing it would still be somewhat formidable.   The government now undertakes to do
a few things, and succeeds in doing them very ill.
Suppose that it should assume the control of all the
industries of the nation : is it reasonable to suppose that
all this vast and complicated work would be well done ?
Let me quote at some length, on this point, from Mr.
Herbert Spencer's essay on "Over Legislation," the whole
of which may be strongly commended to advocates of
" the new socialism : " —

" Did the state fulfil efficiently its unquestionable
duties, there would be some excuse for this eagerness to
assign it further ones.   Were there no complaints of its
faulty administration of justice, of its endless delays and
untold expenses, of its bringing ruin in place of restitution, of its playing the tyrant where it should have been
the protector ; did we never hear of its complicated
stupidities ; its twenty thousand statutes which it assumes
all Englishmen to know, and which not one Englishman
does know ; its multiplied forms which, in the effort to
meet every contingency, open far more loopholes than
they provide against ; had it not shown its folly in
the system of making every alteration by a new act, vari-
ously affecting innumerable preceding acts ; or in its
scores of successive sets of chancery rules, which so
modify and limit and extend and abolish and alter one
another, that not even chancery lawyers know what the

rules are; were we never astounded by such a fact as that, under the system of land-registration in Ireland, six thousand pounds have been spent in a 'negative search' to establish the title of an estate; did we find in its doings no such terrible incongruity as the imprisonment of a hungry vagrant for stealing a turnip, while for the gigantic embezzlements of a railway-director it inflicts no punishment; had we, in short, proved its efficiency as judge and defender, instead of having found it treacherous, cruel, and anxiously to be shunned, — there would be some encouragement to hope other benefits at its hands.

" Or if, while failing in its judicial functions, the state had proved itself a capable agent in some other department, — the military, for example, — there would have been some show of reason for extending its sphere of action. Suppose that it had rationally equipped its troops, instead of giving them cumbrous and ineffective muskets, barbarous grenadier caps, absurdly heavy knapsacks and cartouche-boxes, and clothing colored so as admirably to help the enemy's workmen; suppose that it organized well and economically, instead of salarying an immense superfluity of officers, creating sinecure colonelcies of four thousand pounds a year, neglecting the meritorious, and promoting incapables; suppose that its soldiers were always well housed, instead of being thrust into barracks that invalid hundreds, as at Aden, or that fall on their occupants, as at Loodianah, where ninety-five were thus killed; suppose that in actual war it had shown due administrative ability, instead of occasionally leaving its regiments to march barefoot, to dress in patches, to capture their own engineering tools, and to fight on empty stomachs, as during the peninsular campaign, — suppose all this, and the wish for more state control might still have had some warrant.

" Even though it had bungled in every thing else, yet had it in one case done well, had its naval management alone been efficient, the sanguine would have had a colorable excuse for expecting success in a new field. Grant that the reports about bad ships, ships that will not sail, ships that have to be lengthened, ships with unfit engines, ships that will not carry their guns, ships without stowage, and ships that have to be broken up, are all untrue, . . . and there would remain for the advocates of much government some basis for their political air-castles, spite of military and judicial mismanagement.

" As it is, however, they seem to have read backward the parable of the talents. Not to the agent of proved efficiency do they consign further duties, but to the negligent and blundering agent. Private enterprise has done much, and done it well. Private enterprise has cleared, drained, and fertilized the country, and built the towns; has excavated mines, laid out roads, dug canals, and embanked railways; has invented and brought to perfection ploughs, looms, steam-engines, printing-presses, and machines innumerable; has built our ships, our vast manufactories, our docks; has established banks, insurance societies, and the newspaper press; has covered the sea with lines of steam vessels, and the land with electric telegraphs. Private enterprise has brought agriculture, manufactures, and commerce to their present height, and is now developing them with increasing rapidity. Therefore do not trust private enterprise. On the other hand, the state so fulfils its protective function as to ruin many, delude others, and frighten away those who most need succor; its national defences are so extravagantly and yet inefficiently administered as to call forth almost daily complaint, expostulation, or ridicule; and as the nation's steward it obtains from some of our vast public estates a ruinous revenue. Therefore trust the state. Slight the good and faithful servant, and promote the unprofitable one from one talent to ten.

" Seriously, the case, while it may not in some respects warrant this parallel, is in one respect even stronger; for the new work is not of the same order as the old, but of a more difficult order. Badly as government discharges its true duties, any other duties committed to it are likely to be still worse discharged. To guard its subjects against aggression, either individual or national, is a straightforward and tolerably simple matter: to regulate, directly or indirectly, the personal actions of those subjects, is an infinitely complicated matter. It is one thing to secure to each man the unbounded power to pursue his own good: it is a widely different thing to pursue the good for him. To do the first efficiently, the state has merely to look on while its citizens act, to forbid unfairness, to adjudicate when called on, and to enforce restitution for injuries. To do the last efficiently, it must become an ubiquitous worker, must know each man's needs better than he knows them himself; must, in short, possess superhuman power and intelligence. Even, therefore, had the state done well in its proper sphere, no sufficient warrant would have existed for extending that sphere ; but seeing how ill it has discharged those simple offices which we cannot help consigning to it, small indeed is the probability of its discharging well offices of a more complicated nature." [1]

The charges of inefficiency and wastefulness that Mr. Spencer brings against the government of his own country lie equally against the government of the United States. Neither the monarchy nor the aristocracy of Great Britain is to be blamed for this state of affairs ; for in republican America things are managed just as badly. Indeed, there is good reason to believe that the public service of the mother country is more efficient and less corrupt than that of our own country. " The nation in its collective capacity," or incapacity, has proved itself miserably incompetent to deal with the few interests intrusted to it: the result of putting all " the machinery " of communication, production, and distribution into its hands, and of charging it with the care of all the wealth of the country, may therefore be easily inferred.

Consider what this involves. All the houses not occupied by their owners must pass into the control of the government. The government could not rent them, for rent is robbery : they must therefore be distributed among those who own no houses. On what principle should this allotment be made ? All the railroads and telegraph-lines in the country would belong to the government; all the

[1] "Essays, Moral, Political, and Æsthetic," pp. 51–55.

mills and factories and ships would be owned and operated
by the government; and if I rightly understand "the
new socialism," all the mercantile business of the country
would be transacted by the government. Saying nothing
about the difficulty of managing all these vast affairs by a
political agency, and admitting that they could be thus
managed in such a way as to pay expenses and leave some
surplus for distribution, on what principle should this
distribution be made? "On principles of justice," our
socialistic friends promptly reply. " The present distribution of the proceeds of industry is glaringly unequal: we
insist that they shall be divided equitably." But here
they are not agreed. Three principal methods are formu-
lated by Prof. Cairnes, as finding favor with socialistic
reformers: " To each according to his wants," " To
each according to his works," and, " To each according to
his sacrifices." Let us hear his analysis of these
methods: —

" As regards the first of the formulas to which I have
referred, which proposes to distribute the wealth of a
community among its members in proportion to their
wants, I must frankly acknowledge that I am wholly
unable even to conjecture the method of its application.
How are the wants of individuals to be ascertained? Is
it to be left to each to describe his own wants? And if
the funds are not enough to meet the requirements of all,
who is to decide which is the most urgent? A man with
a large family has greater wants than a man with a small
one. Does this constitute a title to a proportionately

larger share of the proceeds of industry? And, if so, what is to keep the population of a country within the necessary limit of the means of subsistence? Such are some of the questions which meet us on the threshold in seeking to apply this formula, every one of which leads us straight into a *cul de sac.* I must therefore put aside this particular form of the law of distribution, as for me utterly unmanageable. The two latter principles, however, of which one would assign wealth to each person in proportion to the work he has accomplished, and another in proportion to the sacrifice he has undergone, are not at once and obviously impracticable ; and in point of fact, both one and the other do exert, under our existing system of industry, a certain influence in determining the distribution of wealth. For example : wherever the results of industry admit of being measured and compared, as in all work of the same kind, the remuneration of the workman, if any competition is effective, naturally adjusts itself to the results of his work. A workman who in a given time can produce twice as much work as another will in an open market command twice as much wages. But where the results of industry are different in kind, how is the rule of distribution in proportion to the results to be applied? One man in a day produces a coat, another a table, a third superintends a body of workmen : by what result shall we measure these several results, and say that any of them is greater or less than any other ? It is plain that the rule of distribution in proportion to results fails us utterly here. Similarly, the principle of distribution in proportion to sacrifice has also, under our present *régime,* a certain operation in determining the distribution of wealth. But the field of competition, though large, is far from being co-extensive with the industry of any country; and in the absence of competition it is not easy to see how relative sacrifice is to be determined." [1]

If, therefore, the industry of the country thus "nationalized" resulted in any increase of the national wealth, the problem of its distribution would be an extremely difficult one. Our friends the revolutionists ought to have this part of their programme well thought out before they organize their forces for the seizure of the property of their neighbors.

It is only fair to admit, however, that there would be no surplus to divide. Putting the management of all industries into the hands of a national bureaucracy, and excluding from the minds of those who organize labor, as well as of those who perform it, the motive of self-interest, the work would be so poorly managed and so badly done that no gains would be reported at the end of the year. Under the lead of M. Louis Blanc and other socialists, the French republican government, in the days of '48, organized several government workshops, in which a large number of men were employed. These workmen must have a certain daily stipend on which to subsist; and with great prudence the government determined to give them the same wages that they had received under the monarchy, promising to divide the surplus among them. But when the reckoning day came, these shops were found to

[1] "Political Economy," pp. 266, 267.

have made losses rather than profits. This failure was owing quite as much to the indolence and irregularity of the workmen as to the inefficiency of the management. The same result must follow under any system that undertakes to release the workman from the consequences of his own idleness and improvidence, and to put him by force of law into a position which he has failed to gain by his own exertions.

Nothing is surer, therefore, than that the capital of the country thus " nationalized " would rapidly disappear. This capital would never have been accumulated had it not been for the hope entertained by those who now possess it, of keeping it, and enjoying the fruits of it. It cannot be preserved, much less increased, by the operation of any feebler motive. On this subject, hear Prof. Cairnes again : —

" I take it to be a fundamental and indispensable condition of all progressive human society, that by some means or other a large aggregate capital available for its requirements should be provided. Without such a fund, accumulated from the products of past toil, division of labor and continuous industry are impossible ; population cannot attain the degree of density indispensable to civilized existence; nor can that amount of leisure from physical toil be secured for any considerable portion of the people, which is required for the cultivation of science and literature. The maintenance, therefore, of an aggregate capital capable of providing for these requirements, must be regarded as an indispensable condition to be fulfilled by every industrial system which undertakes to promote the well-being and progress of mankind. Now, our economic investigations have shown us that this end — the storing-up of the products of past industry for the purpose of sustaining and assisting present industry — can only be attained at the cost of certain sacrifices ; those sacrifices, namely, implied in foregoing the immediate use of what people have the power of using, and in incurring the risk which attaches in a greater or less degree to all industrial investment. These sacrifices may be regarded as trivial or severe ; but as a matter of fact, they will not be undergone without an adequate motive in the form of a compensating reward. Such a motive our present system of industry provides in the maintenance of private property and industrial freedom. The prospect of profit is the prospect of enjoying as property the results of industrial investment ; and this prospect, under a system of industrial freedom, is thrown open to all who are in the possession of wealth. The inducement thus offered to the acquisitive propensity in man constitutes, under the actual system of things, the ultimate security for all the results which go to form our industrial civilization. The feeling appealed to may, if you like, be a coarse one ; but it is at any rate efficacious ; it *does* lead to habitual and systematic saving, and furnishes society with the necessary material basis for civilized progress. But this motive, every system which annuls private property and freedom of individual industry takes away ; and the question is, What do such systems supply in its place ? Two possible substitutes, so far as I know, and two only, have been or can be suggested, — benevolence and public spirit. I should be very unwilling to disparage such principles of action, or to deny that they are at present extremely influential in public affairs; but I cannot affect to believe that either or that both together — taking human beings not as in the progress of human improvement they may possibly become, but as we now actually find them — could be trusted to supply the place of that desire for individual advancement and well-being to which the institutions of private property and industrial freedom make appeal. I am therefore unable to see how any system which relies upon no stronger or more universal elements of human character than these for its support can fulfil that primary and indispensable condition of all human society, — the providing of a material basis for civilization in the form of an accumulated capital." [1]

This capital which our friends propose to " nationalize " exists, in fact, by virtue of a principle in human nature which they propose to exterminate or repress. I admit, with Mr. Cairnes, that the principle is not the highest upon which human beings can act; but it is the motive power of our material civilization, and any system that undertakes to dispense with it will make small headway. In the millennium, no doubt, disinterested benevolence will lead all the people to labor hard, and live sparingly, in order that their neighbors may be enriched; but in these days very few men have reached this height of virtue, and the great majority will neither be diligent nor prudent

[1] " Political Economy," pp. 271-3.

unless you show them plainly that they can have what they earn, and keep what they save; that they are at liberty to use their accumulated wealth productively in any legitimate industry; that they may exchange it with their neighbors for services, as well as for products; that they may lend it for a lawful or a stipulated remuneration; and that they may give it, when they want it no longer, to whom they will.

Doubtless the possession of capital by their neighbors does seem to some persons a grievous inequality. But this capital represents somebody's savings; and if persons choose to save their money, instead of spending it, they are entitled to some reward for their abstinence. Here are two workmen, each of whom earns eight hundred dollars a year. One of them spends every cent of his earnings: the other denies himself many luxuries, and lays by three hundred dollars every year. Is it not right that the man who has saved the money should be permitted to use it productively; to purchase, for example, a little plot of ground on which he may raise vegetables for the use of his family? Would it not be right even for him to loan his three hundred dollars to another neighbor at a fair rate of interest? He not only foregoes the use of the money himself, but he incurs a certain risk in letting it pass into the hands of another. Is it not fair that he should receive some reward for both these sacrifices?

Yet " the new socialism " in demanding " the nationalization of capital " forbids this thrifty working - man to reap any advantage from his own prudence and self-denial, and insists that he shall either hand over his three hundred dollars every year to the government, or else that he shall tie it up in a napkin or an old stocking, as the case may be, and hide it from the sight of men. A system which thus proscribes individual thrift, and ordains that the man who saves a part of his earnings shall be no better off than the man who consumes them all, will not, I think, commend itself to the favor of intelligent American workmen.

# B.

To prove that socialism is not feasible, is not to conclude that the condition of the laboring-classes under the
present *régime* is what it ought to be. The wages-system
may be better, as men now are, than "the nationalization
of capital;" but under the wages-system, the hardships
of the working-man are many, and his outlook is by no
means cheering. When, therefore, the advocate of "the
new socialism," to whom I have referred in the preceding pages, replies to my criticism of the socialistic methods
by asking "how far the present method of administration
redounds to the equal benefit of the people, or to an
equitable distribution" of the wealth of the country, I
answer frankly, Not to any very satisfactory extent.
That the working-people would, very shortly, be worse
off under a socialistic order than they are at present, I
have no doubt; but this is not to say that they are well
enough off at present. That injustice and inequality bear
heavy rule in their affairs, is altogether too plain. As
Prof. Cairnes has written, "When I look into the
nature of those economic forces, on the play of which the

231

actual distribution of wealth in this and other countries depends, what do I find? Certain physical, physiological, and mental conditions: on the one hand, a productive capacity in the soil, and other natural agents; on the other, certain elements in the character of the people, such as the desire to accumulate wealth and provide for the future, and, constantly counteracting this, a love of present ease and indulgence; lastly, the animal propensities, which continue and multiply the race. These are the forces which, coming into play under a *régime* of private property and freedom of industrial enterprise, determine the proportions in which wealth is divided among a people. But what is there in such circumstances, to make it necessary that the distribution which results shall be in conformity with what our ideas of justice would require? What is there in the case, to secure that the action shall always be in the lines of moral right? The agencies in operation are essentially out of the moral sphere; and if it should, in fact, happen that the results arising from their free action in any given case prove to be in strict accordance with the claims of moral justice, and with so-called 'natural rights,' I do not see that we should be justified in regarding the coincidence as other than a fortunate accident. In point of fact, the practical consequences arising from the conditions of industry in this and other civilized countries are not such as, for my part, I should find it easy to reconcile with any standard of right generally accepted among men."

It must be owned that equity does not rule to any great extent in any of the relations of human beings. How many households are there, in which the members all deal with one another justly? How many social organizations are there, in which impartial justice governs all the members in their treatment of one another? Of what men sometimes call benevolence, there is rather more in the world than of what is rightly called justice. An easy good-nature, a sentimental tenderness, are not so rare as a willingness to respect the rights of others, — their rights of liberty, of property, and of reputation. More people are willing to do me favors than are willing to recognize my rights. Not only in the distribution of wealth, but in all the other affairs of human life, great injustice prevails. Men are not just: the great majority of them are governed in their conduct, not by the principles of equity, but by their selfish interests and passions; and hence these inequalities and hardships which we all deplore. But these traits of human nature will not be eradicated by a new social organization. Give " the nation in its collective capacity" all " the machinery" in the world, and it will not be able to make a single citizen any less extortionate, or any more honorable.

Under no system of industry, therefore, is it reasonable to expect that the wealth of the nation will be equitably distributed, until a vast improvement shall have been wrought in the moral condition of the people; and improvements of this nature are wrought slowly, and not by political agencies.

The evils to which the system of private property and industrial freedom give rise are great; but greater evils would result from its destruction. As human nature now is, the motives to which this system makes appeal are the only adequate motives to industry and prudence. No form of industrial organization will deliver the working-man from all the evils of his condition: but some forms are better than others; and every wise scheme for the improvement of his lot will secure him in the undisturbed possession of his own gains, and in the free use of them. To be a mere laborer, is to live in a dependent condition. He ought to have the opportunity to save his earnings, and to combine the profits realized, from the capital thus saved, with the wages of his labor. A system of industry which identifies the laborer and the capitalist, which gives the workman an immediate interest in the success of the work in which he is engaged, and which secures to him not only the results of his own labor, but also the returns of the capital invested, would seem to enlist all those principles of human nature that have given vigor to our industrial enterprises, while it removes, at least in part, those occasions of conflict by which the progress of industry is so often impeded.

I desire now to give, a little more fully than I was able to do in the foregoing chapters, the arguments and conclusions of some of the most eminent writers of recent times, in support of the system of co-operation. The authorities that I shall cite are within the reach of most working-men; but some of those who read these pages may find my quotations serviceable. First, let me refer again to Prof. Cairnes, whose clear and comprehensive exposition of the whole subject deserves the most careful attention of both working-people and their employers:—

"It appears to me, that the condition of any substantial improvement of a permanent kind in the laborer's lot is, that the separation of industrial classes into laborers and capitalists shall *not* be maintained ; and the laborer shall cease to be a mere laborer, — in a word, that profits shall be brought to re-enforce the wages-fund. . . . Unequal as is the distribution of wealth already in this country, the tendency of industrial progress — on the supposition that the present separation between industrial classes is maintained — is towards an inequality greater still. The rich will be growing richer, and the poor at least relatively poorer. It seems to me, apart altogether from the question of the laborer's interest, that these are not conditions which furnish a solid basis for a progressive social state ; but, having regard to that interest, I think the considerations adduced show that the first and indispensable step toward any serious amendment of the laborer's lot is, that he should be, in one way or other, lifted out of the groove in which he at present works, and placed in a position compatible with his becoming a sharer, in equal proportion with others, in the general advantages arising from industrial progress" (pp. 284, 285).

" The all-important point, as it seems to me, is to recognize the direction in which the emancipation of labor from what is called (absurdly enough) the tyranny of capital lies. This, I repeat, is, and, so far as I can see, only can be, that of co-operative industry. It is, of course, open to any one to question the feasibility of the plan ; to such doubts, the only effective answer, and it has already to some extent been given, will be actual performance ;

but what I think the foregoing argument establishes is, that the alternative lies between this plan and none. If workmen do not rise from dependence upon capital, by the path of co-operation, then they must remain in dependence upon capital. The margin for the possible improvement of their lot is confined within narrow barriers, which cannot be passed; and the problem of their elevation is hopeless. As a body, they will not rise at all. A few, more energetic or more fortunate than the rest, will from time to time escape, as they do now, from the ranks of their fellows, to the higher ranks of industrial life; but the great majority will remain substantially where they are. The remuneration of labor, skilled or unskilled, can never rise much above its present level" (p. 291).

" Co-operation, while it appeals in the strongest way to those attributes of character which are concerned in the control of population, makes comparatively definite and clear the limits of the laborer's resources. He is now a payer as well as a receiver of wages, and, seeing the wages-problem from both sides, is likely to acquire juster views; but even though wages should still remain a mystery, at least it will be tolerably clear that profits will grow with the growth of capital, and that each man may count on receiving them precisely in proportion to the amount of capital he can command. Supposing a workman to have achieved comfortable independence, it will be clear to him, that, to maintain it, he must maintain his capital unimpaired; and that to incur responsibilities which should compel him to encroach upon his capital to meet current expenses, would be tantamount to a deliberate descent in the scale of well-being. The position of the co-operator would in this respect be analogous to that of the present proprietor, who, like him, draws his subsistence from a tolerably definite fund, and generally contrives to keep the expenses of his household within the limits which that fund will support. In these circumstances, it seems to me, there is good ground for hopefulness. Co-operation at once renders less formidable the obstacles to human improvement inevitably incident to our animal propensities, and tends to develop, in those who take part in it, a type of character fitted in a high degree for encountering them with success " (pp. 293, 294).

Prof. Fawcett, in his " Manual of Political Economy," p. 279, says of this method of industry, " Any one who considers what it has already effected, and what it is capable of doing in the future, must, we think, come to the conclusion that we may look with more confidence to co-operation than to any other economic agency to improve the industrial condition of the country."

Lord Derby's opinions are cited on p. 208. Let me quote a little more fully, from Mr. Thomas Brassey's " Work and Wages," p. 259, the words of the noble lord : " It is human nature that a man should like to feel that he is to be the gainer by any extra industry that he may put forth ; that he would like to have some sense of proprietorship in a shop or a mill, or whatever it may be, in which he spends his days ; and it is because the system, introduced of late years, of co-operative industry, meets this natural wish, that I look forward to its extension with so much hopefulness. I believe it is the best and surest remedy for that antagonism of labor and capital which we hear so much talk of, and which to a certain extent no doubt exists. . . . I am well aware that such a state of things as I have pointed out cannot be brought about in a day. It is quite probable that there are some trades and some kinds of business in which it cannot be brought about at all ; but it seems to me that it is in this direction that the efforts of the best workers and the ideas of the best thinkers are tending : and we are not to be disappointed because we do not hit at once upon the best way of doing what has never been done before."

Mr. John Stuart Mill, in his chapter on " The Probable Future of the Laboring-Classes," gives an excellent account of what had been accomplished in this direction at the time of his writing, reaching this conclusion : " If the improvement which even triumphant military despotism has only retarded, not stopped, shall continue its course, there can be little doubt that the *status* of hired laborers will gradually tend to confine itself to the description of work-people whose low moral qualities render them unfit for any thing more independent ; and that the relation of masters and work-people will be gradually superseded by partnership in one of two forms, — in some cases, association of the laborers with the capitalist ; in others, and perhaps finally in all, association of laborers among themselves." [1]

The fact adverted to by Mr. Mill, that co-operation demands of those who enter upon it some degree of intel-

---

[1] " Principles of Political Economy," People's Edition, p. 461.

ligence and moral development, is insisted upon by Prof. Cairnes and by all the writers who favor the method.

Mr. Brassey, an experienced contractor and a careful student of the labor question, in an article in " The Contemporary Review " of July, 1874, makes one or two practical suggestions to which intending co-operators will do well to take heed : " It is because there has been in co-operative establishments a reluctance to pay what is necessary to enlist first-rate ability in the management of the business, that their operations have been attended hitherto with very partial success. Only personal experience of the difficulties of the task would induce a body of workmen to reserve from their earnings a sum sufficient to secure the services of competent leaders. We would therefore earnestly advise those interested in co-operative production to discourage attempts to commence on a large scale a business difficult to manage. A moderate capital is easily obtained. Large funds are not rapidly procured. When only a few hands are engaged, the government may be conducted on a purely democratic basis. Where the energies of a multitude are combined, there must be an enlightened despotism. . . . When the business is of a kind that cannot be carried out advantageously on a moderate footing, the co-operative principle should be applied to the execution of sub-contracts for portions of the work, to the supply of a part of a large order, or to the execution of a single process in a complicated manufacture."

The question of procuring the capital for these industrial operations is referred to by Mr. Brassey; and it is just here that the socialistic theorists demand help from the government. The newspaper critic to whose observations attention has been given in this Appendix declares that the author of this volume " makes a terrible mistake in supposing that any material improvement will take place in the condition of the working-classes through their becoming capitalists by means of their own savings." I can only turn the point of this sentence, and say that a terrible mistake is made by any man who supposes that their physical condition can be improved in any other way. Practically, capital can be obtained by those who do not inherit it, in only two ways : by saving their earnings, and by robbery. That it is a terrible mistake to steal, even when it is done under the forms of law, I am very sure. But the difficulty of honestly acquiring capital, on the part of working-men, is by no means so great as some of their counsellors would make them believe. Let us hear one more wise word on this point from Prof. Cairnes : " If, then, the laborer is to emerge from his present position, and become a sharer in the gains of capital, he must in the first instance learn to save. To make saving practicable, it is true, there must be a margin of income beyond what is required for providing the necessaries of life ; and I shall perhaps be told that this margin the laborer does not possess. But this is an assertion which cannot for a moment be maintained in the face of the evidence furnished by the excise returns. From these returns it has been calculated that a ·sum of no less than one hundred and twenty million pounds sterling is now spent annually on alcoholic drinks. [It will be remembered that the report of the Bureau of Statistics, as quoted on one of the foregoing pages, gives about the same amount, six hundred million dollars, as the sum expended for the same purpose in the United States.] In what proportion the working-classes take part in this expenditure, we have no means of accurately determining ; but I imagine it will not be disputed, that by much the larger proportion must be set down to their account ; and I am certainly within the mark in assuming, that of the money so spent, I am sure I might say three-fourths of the whole, so far from conducing in any way to the well-being of those who spend it, is both physically and morally injurious to them. Here, then, is a sum of, let us say, sixty million pounds sterling, which might annually be saved without trenching upon any expenditure which really contributes to the laborer's well-being. The obstacles to this saving are not physical but moral obstacles, and supposing laborers had the virtue to overcome them, the first step toward what might be called their industrial emancipation would already have been accomplished " (pp. 287, 288).

16

**DATE DUE**

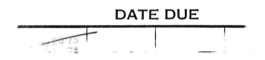